PRIDE, SHAME, AND GUILT

Pride, Shame, and Guilt

Emotions of self-assessment

GABRIELE TAYLOR

CLARENDON PRESS · OXFORD
1985

Oxford University Press, Walton Street, Oxford OX2 6DP

Oxford New York Toronto
Delhi Bombay Calcutta Madras Karachi
Kuala Lumpur Singapore Hong Kong Tokyo
Nairobi Dar es Salaam Cape Town
Melbourne Auckland

and associated companies in
Beirut Berlin Ibadan Mexico City Nicosia

Oxford is a trade mark of Oxford University Press

Published in the United States
by Oxford University Press, New York

British Library Cataloguing in Publication Data

Taylor, Gabrielle
Pride, shame and guilt:
emotions of self-assessment.
1. Emotions   2. Self-perception
I. Title
152.4   BF531
ISBN 0-19-824620-X

Set by DMB (Typesetting), Oxford
Printed in Great Britain
at the University Press, Oxford
by David Stanford
Printer to the University

ACKNOWLEDGEMENTS

———♦•••♦———

AMONG the friends who over the years have greatly encouraged me by their interest in and discussion of the various topics, I should like to thank particularly Kathleen Lennon and Patricia Ingham. I am very grateful to Philippa Foot for her meticulous care in reading the typescript and her help in removing many inaccuracies.

Earlier and rather different versions of 'Pride' and 'Integrity' were published in *Explaining Emotions*, ed. Amélie Oksenberg Rorty (University of California Press, 1980) and *The Aristotelian Society* Supplementary Volume 1981, respectively.

CONTENTS

I

EMOTIONS AND BELIEFS

IN the chapters to come I shall discuss a number of particular emotions which can be collected together under the label 'emotions of self-assessment'. Examples of members of this group are pride, humiliation, shame, and guilt. There is of course no one principle according to which different emotions can be classified and labelled;[1] how they are collected will depend largely on the purpose and interest of the collector. The interest of the emotions of self-assessment, for the philosopher at least, lies primarily in the nature and complexity of the beliefs involved. It is because they resemble each other in requiring the same sorts of beliefs that they can be treated as one group, and it is because of the nature of these beliefs that the label is appropriate: in experiencing any one of these emotions the person concerned believes of herself that she has deviated from some norm and that in doing so she has altered her standing in the world. The self is the 'object' of these emotions, and what is believed amounts to an assessment of that self.

It is plain from these remarks that the analysis of emotions here offered will be in terms of beliefs.[2] This is not to claim that all emotions should always be analysed in these terms. Nor is it

---

[1] The most familiar classifications are no doubt Spinoza's active or passive emotions, and Hume's direct or indirect passions. Sometimes we single out 'moral' or 'social' emotions. But many other ways of classifying are available, e.g. emotions which are cross-cultural in origin and expression against those which are not; those which can be physiologically induced, those which are primarily dispositional rather than occurrent, and so on (see Amélie Oksenberg Rorty's Introduction to *Explaining Emotions*, University of California Press, 1980).

[2] For discussions of emotions in terms of beliefs see for example R. Scruton, 'Attitudes, Beliefs and Reasons' in J. Casey, ed., *Morality and Moral Reasoning* (Methuen, 1971); J. R. Wilson, *Emotion and Object* (Cambridge University Press, 1972); R. M. Gordon, 'The Aboutness of Emotion', *American Philosophical Quarterly* xi, 1 (January 1974); I. Thalberg, *Perception, Emotion and Action* (Basil Blackwell, 1977).

to claim that where the analysis in terms of beliefs is applicable it is also exhaustive. A complete account would normally include consideration of other features, such as wants and wishes, sensations and physiological changes. Over a wide range of emotions, however, beliefs are constitutive of the emotional experience in question. They are constitutive in two ways. Firstly, one (or more) of the beliefs makes the emotional experience what it is, it identifies it as, for example, anger, and so differentiates it from other states, such as jealousy or envy. But secondly, there will also be further beliefs because of which the person experiencing the emotion will hold the identificatory belief(s). These are constitutive of the emotion in that they are causally responsible for it being what it is: I hold the first, identificatory belief only because I hold this second belief(s). Normally, if I feel fear, for example, then I believe the situation confronting me to be dangerous or harmful, and I believe this because I believe that it has some particular characteristic in virtue of which it is harmful. I am afraid of the snake because its bite is poisonous and poison would harm me.

The beliefs which are constitutive of the emotional experience are thereby also explanatory. They explain in that they give the person's reasons for being in a certain state. Not all references to a person's beliefs explain in just this way: the given belief may causally explain without giving a reason. I may, for instance, cite some childhood experience in explanation of my present fear of the snake. In that case I should not be offering an explanation which gives my reasons for feeling afraid. Reference to my earlier experience may or may not explain my present state. Whether it does or not is not at all dependent on my believing either that I had such an experience or that there is a link between it and what I am feeling now. It may provide an explanation irrespective of who holds these beliefs. But if the explanation is to be seen as giving the person's reasons, the beliefs referred to must be hers, or must at least be assumed to be hers. Nor does the present type of explanation make any appeal to rationality. I may admit that although afraid of it I believe the snake in front of me to be perfectly harmless or safely behind glass. My fear does not seem to have a reason, and the reference to my childhood experience is an attempt to explain my irrational fear. Since I do not believe the snake to be dangerous I do not hold the relevant identificatory belief and hence hold no beliefs on which the identificatory belief would depend.[3]

This type of causal explanation is to be distinguished from that in which what is explained is the identificatory belief itself, and where (consequently) reference to the agent's beliefs is crucial and not merely accidental. These beliefs are the agent's reasons for holding the identificatory belief, and they are explanatory of his state not just because of their content, but because they are the agent's beliefs. The content and the fact that this content is believed by him cannot, for explanatory purposes, be taken apart as it could be in the case of the first type of explanation. His fear of the snake is now explained and so made intelligible if we understand that he believes, rightly or wrongly, its bite to be poisonous, and that it is dangerous because poisonous. If he does not believe these two features to be causally connected then that it is poisonous is not his reason for, and so cannot explain, his belief that the snake is dangerous. For an emotional state to be intelligible in this second sense it is necessary at least to impute the relevant beliefs to the person concerned.[4]

The second type of explanation, unlike the first, aims at making the emotional state rationally intelligible. The reasons given by the agent's beliefs are meant to explain rationally his identificatory belief, and so rationally explain the state itself. As a rational explanation the beliefs offered may of course be more or less successful. They may or may not be well-founded, they may or may not be justified in the light of

---

[3] Fear, then, does not always seem to require explanatory beliefs (my fear of the dark) nor even always require an identificatory belief (my fear of the spider which I know to be harmless). Scruton ('Attitudes, Beliefs and Reasons', p. 35) says that since this belief (that some object is harmful) is present in *every* case of fear, as a matter of logic, we cannot talk of fear except when there is this belief. But we do speak of fear in cases where his condition is not satisfied and it seems arbitrary to hold that this description is misapplied. Perhaps in cases where what he calls the 'reactive content' of the emotion is sufficiently similar to that of fear in a situation believed to be harmful we can speak of the person as feeling fear, although he lacks the relevant belief. In that case it would still be true that this use of 'fear' is parasitic on the standard use of the term, for we could not speak of him as feeling fear on the basis of his reactions alone unless the reactions are those normally associated with the belief 'this is harmful'; otherwise we should have no means of identifying them as *fear*-reactions.

[4] See Donald Davidson, 'Hume's Cognitive Theory of Pride', *Journal of Philosophy*, Vol. lxxiii, No. 19 (November 1976).

what the circumstances actually are. Even if the beliefs about the given situation are correct and justified, it may be open to doubt whether its particular characteristics are such that they make it, for example, dangerous. The snake, though poisonous, is a retiring creature and so quite unlikely to bite. All the reasons offered, and therefore the emotional experience itself, can be evaluated in the light of available evidence.

The example I have chosen to illustrate the role of beliefs as making the emotional experience rationally intelligible was an exceedingly simple one, and the beliefs therefore easy to assess. I have spoken as if the function of the different kinds of belief, identificatory and explanatory, can always be neatly separated, so that given only the identificatory belief it is settled that the person concerned is experiencing some particular emotion, and this particular experience may or may not become intelligible depending on what reasons (if any) for this state can be produced. But this is far too simple a picture; there is not always such clear demarcation between the identification and the intelligibility of an emotional state. Sometimes it is relatively easy to keep them apart. This tends to be so in cases like fear when the non-cognitive features, the behavioural and physiological reactions, are often prominent and not difficult to recognize. It may not be possible to doubt that I believe myself to be confronted by something dangerous, even though there may be no reason for this belief that I or others can spell out. But in the case of other emotions where there is either little non-cognitive reaction, or where such reaction is not more typical of one emotion than of another, the identification of the emotion may be questioned or rejected unless it is backed by explanatory reasons. In such a case the suggested identificatory belief may not be accepted as genuine.

My example of the poisonous snake was simple also in that the fear was perfectly intelligible and presented no particular problems of justification. If the snake really is poisonous, or if there are good grounds for believing it to be, then there is at least some reason for feeling fear, for poison just is harmful to human beings. (This of course is not to say that giving in to fear can necessarily be justified.) Other emotions, or other occurrences of fear, may need more, or more complex, beliefs to become intelligible, and what constitutes evidence for or against the rationality of some belief is often not easy, or is even impossible to settle. Given that what is to be explained and assessed is an emotional state, the person concerned must in some way be affected by the situation, otherwise she would not be experiencing an emotion. This means that (roughly) she will have an either favourable or unfavourable attitude towards it, and this attitude will be reflected in her beliefs. Justifying such attitude-beliefs may well involve reference to some framework which itself will need defence, and such a defence will pose particular problems where the framework is a moral one or has moral implications. So, for example, a duchess's indignation at being treated so casually may be justifiable only given acceptance of some hierarchical order which alots a special status to members of the aristocracy.

In the discussion of the emotions of self-assessment I shall concentrate on the relevant beliefs involved in so far as they are explanatory in the second sense, as making the emotional experience rationally intelligible. I shall therefore offer identificatory and explanatory beliefs on the basis of which it should be at least theoretically possible to assess the reasonableness or otherwise of experiencing a particular emotion on a particular occasion. There is, however, still the need to settle how rational intelligibility can be made to be, given that we are dealing with emotional experience of individuals who may hold quite different beliefs about the same situation, supposing that situation to be objectively described. In the remainder of this chapter I shall consider the account of rational intelligibility suggested by Davidson. His account, it seems to me, insists on a form of rationality which is not illuminating in the context, and which is not necessary for an understanding and assessment of the emotional experience in question. In his paper 'Hume's Cognitive Theory of Pride' Davidson discusses what he calls 'propositional emotions' (Hume's 'indirect passions'), which are those emotions where reason-giving is appropriate. His example of such an emotion is pride, to which Hume of course paid particular attention. But shame or guilt as well as many other emotions would fall into this group. Davidson's claim is that the set of beliefs which are explanatory of the emotion in question must include one which is universal in form. This at least is the interpretation suggested by the basic structure of pride which he offers. In Davidson's account of pride we have, firstly, a belief concerning oneself, that one owns something, has a certain characteristic, or stands in some relationship to someone else. Secondly, there is an attitude of approbation or esteem for anyone who has this characteristic. Together these result in, i.e., are causally responsible for, the self-approval or self-esteem which, he thinks, is normally called pride. 'The causes of pride are thus judgments which logically imply the judgment that is identical with pride', he says (p. 751). So we have a syllogism: if a person is proud of his beautiful house then he believes that (i) he owns a beautiful house, that (ii) owners of beautiful houses are praiseworthy (in so far as they own beautiful houses), and so (iii) that *he* is praiseworthy (in so far as he owns a beautiful house). The last belief expresses the emotion. The first two beliefs both cause and give that person's reasons for his pride.

There is evidently much here that is similar to my earlier account of fear of the snake. The relation between the beliefs was also causal, and also such that in citing them we give the person's reason for his fear. But Davidson insists on the introduction of a universal, and it is on this aspect of his account that I wish to concentrate. I think it is a mistaken move.

The point of the explanatory account in terms of beliefs is to make the person's state intelligible. The suggestion now is that for this to be achieved a belief which is universal in form is to be included in the explanation. The introduction of a universal enables Davidson to put the required explanation in the form of a syllogism, so that the reasoning which leads the person to the conclusion that he is praiseworthy in a certain respect is deductive reasoning. The underlying assumption here seems to be that an explanation of the belief that p in terms of the person's reasons q and r makes p intelligible if and only if reasons q and r are logically sufficient for p, so that given he believes that q and r he must, as a rational being, also believe that p, for p is entailed by the conjunction of q and r. If there is a gap, if there is no such entailment, it is left partially obscure just why he believes that p.

This is not an implausible view. It is fair enough to suggest that if I believe this snake will harm me because it is poisonous then I am now also committed to the belief that poisonous snakes are harmful. Maybe I do not think that all such snakes harm, but I can qualify my belief without undermining the universal: snakes whose bite is very poisonous harm, or poisonous snakes which bite at the slightest provocation harm, etc. The first universal proposition is not adequate merely because it had not been spelt out properly, but as soon as I am more specific about the features which in my view make the situation harmful I again have a suitable universal. The only escape from the universal seems to be a refusal on my part to articulate fully just what I regard as harmful: there is just something about *this* snake which makes me afraid. In that case I have not provided sufficient conditions for harmfulness on which a universal can be based. But it can also be said with justice that my fear remains obscure.

This consideration yields the principle that if a person's belief that p is to be made fully intelligible it must be entailed by other beliefs, which for present purposes we take as given; and this means that at least one of these beliefs must be universal.

I do not wish to deny that a belief which is universal in form can always be found when explaining an emotional state, and this universal may indeed contribute towards making the experience intelligible. My objection to the principle just stated is that the universal may not always play this role. The reason for the objection is this: to make intelligible a person's belief that p ('I am praiseworthy') given that he believes that r ('I own a beautiful house') we must make explicit the reasoning which makes his belief that r a reason for his belief that p, and makes it that from which his belief that p results. If this is made explicit by his belief that q, then this belief, universal or otherwise, must constitute a step in his reasoning.

So we also have this principle: if the belief that q is to make intelligible the belief that p then it must be a step in the reasoning which explains the belief that p, otherwise it has no role to play in the explanation. So where the belief that q is a belief which is universal in form, the universal must have this explanatory role. If it fails to do so then the object of the exercise, viz., to provide an explanation of the person's state, is frustrated. Therefore, to show that it is a mistake to require that one of the agent's relevant beliefs be a universal it will be sufficient to show that a suitable universal in a given situation may fail to comply with this second principle of intelligibility. It is a consequence of this possibility that the first principle given, plausible though it may seem, is nevertheless unacceptable.

I shall illustrate my claim with a case of humiliation. Like pride, humiliation is what Davidson calls a 'propositional emotion' in that here, too, reason-giving is appropriate. So it should fit the Davidson scheme. In introducing a more complex example I hope to show that his account is too neat and too simple. The case it fits best is the one where the person concerned already holds the view that, for example, owners of beautiful houses are praiseworthy. Now, finding himself in possession of a beautiful house, he applies this general view to the particular case in hand. This is, of course, a possible state of affairs. But alternatively he may come to formulate his views on owners of beautiful houses when contemplating his own position as house-owner. In such a case it is rather more doubtful that any universal that may emerge has an explanatory function. It may not have sufficient substance to do so. This point connects with another: the syllogistic pattern forces on us the view of intelligibility I have outlined, and which to some extent is a plausible one. But surely only to some extent. For it may be the case that a detailed explanation in terms of particular beliefs may make the person's belief that p intelligible in a much more satisfactory way. It is not so much that we come to see that as a rational being he must believe that p if he also believes that q and r; we may come to understand rather that this particular person at this particular time would naturally react to the situation in the way he does. And this we may come to understand not by linking his assessment of the situation to other, similar ones, thus yielding a belief of the type 'owners of beautiful houses are praiseworthy', but by learning more about his particular beliefs about this and perhaps other situations.

The case of humiliation I shall use to illustrate these points is taken from James Joyce's short story 'The Dead'.[5] The protagonist, Gabriel, has spent the evening at a party given by his aunts, where his function was to see that all went smoothly, and to make the after-dinner speech. He is now alone with his

---

[5] In *Dubliners* (Penguin Modern Classics, 1956), pp. 173–220.

wife Gretta and has just been listening to her reminiscences. She has been telling him of a boy, a boy employed in the gasworks, who years ago was in love with her and who died, she thinks, for her sake. Gabriel tries to stop her telling the tale by making ironic comments, but she does not even notice that this is what he is doing. This is his reaction:

Gabriel felt humiliated by the failure of his irony and by the evocation of this figure from the dead, a boy in the gasworks. While he had been full of memories of their secret life together, full of tenderness and joy and desire, she had been comparing him in her mind with another. A shameful consciousness of his own person assailed him. He saw himself as a ludicrous figure, acting as a penny-boy for his aunts, a nervous, well-meaning sentimentalist, orating to vulgarians and idealizing on his own clownish lusts, the pitiable fatuous fellow he had caught a glimpse of in the mirror.   (pp. 216–7.)

Gabriel's reaction has the sort of complexity which often characterizes emotional situations. It is typical of humiliation that it spreads from the present occasion to other aspects of one's life. Gabriel goes through a series of humiliations, and he is nicely articulate about them, or Joyce is so for him. Several suggestions as to why he feels as he does, i.e., what his reasons for his state are, can be extracted from the passage. First, Gabriel thinks the situation humiliating because, he believes, his irony failed and Gretta evoked that figure from the dead, the boy in the gasworks. This, taken in isolation, is not enough to make his state wholly intelligible, but the relevant universal 'situations like the one described are humiliating' would not be a particularly explanatory belief to produce, nor is there any reason to think that this would be Gabriel's attitude in general to situations of this kind. He may think that sometimes a situation under the given description reflects not on the listener to the story, but on the teller of it: Gretta should have seen his piece of irony for what it was and snapped out of her mood. So the situation as described may sometimes be irritating to Gabriel, rather than humiliating. There is a particular difficulty about the dead being a boy from the gasworks, which for Gabriel seems to be the last straw, but which in universalized form would look just silly. And if he held the (surely insane) view that these kinds of situation are particularly humiliating whenever the figure evoked is a boy from the gasworks then this would hardly add to our understanding of Gabriel's reaction, for that would require rather that we see the point of the boy's occupation being so grating.

But maybe it is the next sentence we should pick out as giving the crucial reason for his feeling humiliated, and as therefore affording better grounds for a universal. If so, then he should now believe this type of situation mortifying: he (any he) is full of memories of their secret life together while she compares him in her mind with another. But again, why should Gabriel commit himself to the truth of such a general belief? He may be quite aware that a person of greater generosity and with less concern with his own image may well not take such a view of the case. Still, it may be that the universal has not been properly stated. Perhaps we should add that it is only for people like Gabriel in relevant respects that such a situation is humiliating. But this is not a step in the right direction: the universal must be a belief of his which constitutes a step in his reasoning and so helps to explain his state. To be at all explanatory the 'relevant respects' clause has to be filled in. The most likely reading would be something of this sort: self-centred, non-confident people will be humiliated in such circumstances. However, the belief that he has a certain character, that he is the person he is, is as little a step in the reasoning which leads him to think the situation humiliating as the belief 'I had such-and-such an experience in my childhood' would be. Such a belief may conceivably explain why he tends to see situations as humiliating when others do not; it does not explain in virtue of what features he sees the situation in this light, and therefore does not contribute to the rational intelligibility of the experience.

The passage quoted makes it quite clear that Gabriel becomes aware of a whole pattern in his behaviour in different areas: it is all of a piece that he cuts a sorry figure as a husband, a nephew and orator. His present experience makes him take a certain view of himself which goes beyond the given context. But the connection also holds the other way: it may well be that he takes Gretta's reminiscences in the way he does only because of incidents which occurred earlier in the evening. Had he not (in his own view) dealt inadequately with a number of

other encounters then he might still have felt sad or upset by
the Gretta situation as her mood did not accord with his, but he
might not have felt humiliated. So maybe a suitably explanatory universal would have to be of roughly this sort: 'for someone who already thinks of himself as inadequate in other
respects, the present situation is mortifying'. But this again is
not explanatory in the way required as it again does not give us
his reason for his state.

Nevertheless, it is against the background of his earlier experiences, against, that is, the background of his particular
beliefs about earlier situations, that his beliefs about the present
situation make his humiliation intelligible, though none of
those beliefs function as his reasons for seeing the situation as
he does. Maybe in such a tangled case the kind of intelligibility
Davidson had in mind just cannot be had. Certainly, Gabriel's
particular beliefs about the situation so far discussed do not
fully explain his state. But the introduction of a universal
would not solve the problem. I have tried to show that there
would be no irrationality in Gabriel's refusal to commit himself
to the truth of the relevant belief which is universal in form.
But even if he were so committed we should not have gained in
understanding, for the universal would be totally concocted out
of his particular beliefs. This being so it could hardly perform a
role in the explanation of his state which is not already performed by his particular beliefs. It would be wholly derivative
and so superfluous.

It would, however, not be correct to say that none of Gabriel's
beliefs commit him to the relevant universal. In the second part
of the passage we are given some of his beliefs which do so commit him. Gabriel thinks it humiliating that he has orated to
vulgarians and idealized his clownish lusts. In believing this he
is so committed because he has to believe in all consistency that
situations so described are humiliating, and he has to believe
this in all consistency because that such a situation is humiliating is built into the description of that situation. It is slanted in
such a way that only someone who sees the situation as humiliating would describe it in these terms. It is because Gabriel
formulates his beliefs in these terms that they identify his state
of mind as one of humiliation. Talking or chatting to vulgarians
may be entertaining or boring or quite without significance.

But *orating* to vulgarians is a different matter: only a pompous ass would do that. Similarly, to think of one's lusts as 'clownish', and to think of oneself as idealizing them under this description cannot but express one's contempt for them and for oneself. Where a way of describing a situation entails this situation being seen as affecting the person concerned in a certain way, it will of course always be the case that whenever that person thinks the description applicable he will be affected in that way. But that Gabriel can be said to hold a universal belief of that kind is of no explanatory use whatever, for it is entirely trivial.

The point to be extracted from the case of Gabriel is a quite general one: some universal belief which we can ascribe to the agent on grounds of consistency alone can no doubt always be found. But this is often unlikely to be sufficiently substantial to be at all explanatory. On the other hand, the ascription of a substantial belief which is universal rests on the sometimes unjustified assumption that the agent in describing the relevant features of the present situation has thereby picked out a set of conditions which he must regard as sufficient for the assessing of situations of this kind as, for instance, praiseworthy or mortifying, so that he now has a rule whereby he can pick out other situations as falling under this description. But this is only sometimes the case. For the agent may be aware (or become aware when he thinks about the matter) that it is only because of very particular circumstances that he connects certain features of the situation with its being praiseworthy, degrading, or whatever.

The function of the agent's beliefs was to explain his emotional state and make it intelligible. The question now arises whether the removal of a belief which is universal in form would undermine this function, whether in doing so I am perhaps left with something quite unexplained, a Humean atomic feeling maybe, which we just cannot get at. This is just the sort of thing Davidson wants to get rid of:

Hume surely did often, and characteristically, assert that a pleasant feeling, or a feeling of pleasure of a certain sort, was essential to pride, whereas no such feeling is essential; and, more important, such an element does not help in analyzing an attitude of approval, or a judgment. (p. 754.)

The first point to make in response to this kind of worry is that of course the detailed examination of my example was designed to show that the intelligibility achieved by the introduction of a universal belief does not always amount to much, so that dropping this requirement will not always be a loss. The second point is to concede that yes, an explanation in terms of beliefs may not always make the agent's state wholly intelligible. This is perhaps an advantage, emotions being what they are. Davidson's account does seem to over-intellectualize the emotions. It is not necessary to accept his scheme if one wants to avoid being left with a state of mind or feeling which it is impossible to get hold of. On my account it can after all be identified by a suitable description of the agent's particular beliefs about the situation, as Gabriel's feelings of humiliation were identified in the last part of the quoted passage. And the final point to make is that I have in my account sufficient constraints of rationality to ensure intelligibility in many cases. Apart from normal constraints of consistency there is also the requirement that, for his state to be intelligible, his particular beliefs about the situation must fit the description which is identificatory of the emotion in question; it has to be the case that where a person is, for example, afraid of something his particular beliefs about that thing are such that they explain why (in his view) it is harmful to him. But there may be no simple or obvious way of doing this, such as establishing an entailment relation between his various beliefs. We may rather come to see the point of his connecting one belief with another when we understand more about the agent's pattern of beliefs of which this connection is a part, and such a pattern may become clearer to us when we learn how he views other situations, or how he sees himself as an agent trying to cope under different circumstances. That is to say, to grasp his reason for feeling fear or pride or humiliation we may have to go beyond his beliefs about the situation, for it may not be clear why these are reasons for his state unless we take into account other beliefs of his. Knowledge of Gabriel's attitude to earlier events, to his having to make the speech, to the taunts of a colleague or the remark of a servant-girl, is of much greater help in understanding his humiliation in the scene described than would be any universal belief ascribed to him.

If 'rational intelligibility' implies the kind of deductive reasoning Davidson suggests, then I am now speaking of a different, or additional, kind of intelligibility. It is still rational, in that the explanation is in terms of the agent's reasons for his identificatory belief, and these reasons in turn are open to rational assessment. It is also rational in the sense that we can impute to the agent all those beliefs he must hold in all consistency, given he holds certain beliefs about the situation. But the (universal) beliefs which he must hold in all consistency need not constitute a step in his reasoning and need not add to the explanation of his state. The additional explanatory factor I am now introducing is also not a step in his reasoning leading to the identificatory belief; it is not in this sense a rational element. The reference to other particular beliefs of the agent's in other particular situations make his present state intelligible to us because they make us understand why his present beliefs constitute his reasons for his emotional experience. At this point the constraints on what is explanatory are not provided by what must be the case in all rationality. The appeal is no longer to the wholly rational being; it is to the admittedly far less neat and precise notion of what it would be human and natural for a person to feel under certain circumstances, given that person's relevant other beliefs and attitudes.

I spoke earlier of the variety of beliefs involved in emotional experience, some of which will express a favourable or unfavourable attitude towards the situation, a positive or negative evaluation. Such beliefs will be more or less difficult to assess, and indeed to understand, depending on the nature of the relevant framework. The difficulty may not be great if such a framework is 'objective' in the sense of being shared by a society or by all 'normal' human beings. But it may also be a very individual one. The more individual the 'framework' (if this is what it can still be called) the less plausible it is to speak of the situation to which the agent reacts as if it could be described in terms which are independent of his beliefs about it. Such a description is of course always available, but it may contribute very little to an explanation of his state. The beliefs, respectively, of the man afraid of the snake and of Gabriel humiliated by Gretta's behaviour illustrate this point: that a poisonous snake is dangerous is an easily understood and acceptable fact;

that the evocation of the boy in the gasworks is humiliating, is not. Emotions of self-assessment tend to present the complexities of the latter case. This is so because the person experiencing such an emotion does not just see the situation in evaluative terms, he also assimilates what he values or disvalues into a structure of his achievements or failures, as so viewed by him. We therefore have here different dimensions of interconnected assessment: his evaluation of the situation will cause him to alter his view of himself to a lesser or greater degree, though perhaps only temporarily. But also conversely, it is at least very likely that he evaluates the situation as he does because his view of himself is what it is.

It follows from the nature of the relevant beliefs that a person who gives little thought to his own conduct and aims, or to how in different situations one should or should not react, will not be much assailed by such emotions. And it also follows from the nature of these beliefs that if, having given thought to the situation, he thinks that all is as it should be, that he gets what he expects and himself contributes what is expected of him, he, too, will not be much involved in the drama of experiencing such emotions. To speak of 'drama' here is not inappropriate. In essence, a dramatic situation in a play is a happening which brings about a change for all concerned, as does for instance the tale of the Messenger in Sophocles' *Oedipus*, which was meant to reassure but instead reveals the secret of the king's birth and so has disastrous consequences.[6] What has been discovered about Oedipus alters his position completely. The experience of an emotion of self-assessment is also a happening which changes the state of things. The change is in the view the agent takes of himself. Starting from a set of beliefs or assumptions about himself, his conception of some event or state of affairs is such that he has to formulate beliefs about himself which conflict with the ones held initially; so he has to alter his view of himself. This consequent view may be fleeting only and not make much impression; whether it does or not depends partly on how important he judges the event or state of affairs to be, and partly on his view when more detached as to how

[6] This is the example Aristotle uses to illustrate peripety and discovery, *De Poetica* 1452a.

justified he was in giving it that degree of importance. Gabriel undergoes such a change when listening to Gretta's story of the boy in the gasworks. He sees the situation as Gretta comparing him with another, a comparison which is not flattering to himself. Consequently, he is forced to take a view of himself and of his relationship with her which is different and more pessimistic than the one he held or unthinkingly assumed just before this event. The new situation, as seen by him, clashes with the world as he (possibly unthinkingly) expected to find it, and as a result there is a change in his beliefs concerning this relationship to this world, and thereby also concerning himself. He now sees it as quite different from what he took it to be, and this difference is reflected in his own standing. The drama is of course internal: the view of the event is the agent's and the change takes place within him. He provides the stage as well as the *dramatis personae*.

Someone prone to such emotions no doubt leads in this respect a more exciting and exhausting life than those comparatively immune to them. Whether or not he leads a more or less admirable life cannot of course be settled *in vacuo*. Much will depend on whether the beliefs involved in the emotional response, or for that matter involved in the lack of such response, are at all justified or not. In some cases the experiencing of these emotions may indicate a degree of moral sensitivity which he who does not experience them on similar occasions may lack; in others it may betray an undue preoccupation with his own importance. Much will also depend on what the agent makes of his experience. In trying to find out why he feels pride or guilt or shame on this or that occasion he may make discoveries about himself which may change his whole outlook and lead him to form a different and perhaps juster view of himself and of the life which he should lead. But whatever the case, it is clear at any rate that an investigation of this group of emotions will have a bearing on the assessment of people as moral agents.

II

———◆———

PRIDE AND HUMILITY

1

A proud man, the dictionary tells us, is one who values himself highly on account of his rank, position, or possessions. The humble man, by contrast, is said to have a low opinion of himself. One might think of them as occupying two positions at the opposite ends of some scale. A person can then be said to be humble simply in virtue of his occupying a humble or lowly position, quite independently of any feelings he may have about the situation. We do not use 'proud' as a label for those at the other end of the scale, but we can refer to them as 'the noble' in virtue of their occupying such a high position. This characterization assumes a system by reference to which high and low positions can be defined. The most obvious example is a hierarchical social system, like the feudal system of the Middle Ages.

Whoever occupies some position in such a system may or may not be aware of his relative standing on the scale. If he is unaware of it, then the question of how he views the situation does not arise. His position is humble or noble independently of his view of it; it is objectively so, given the system. If he is aware of his objective relative position and gives any thought to the matter then he may either accept it as his due, or he may reject it as being higher or lower than is due to him. It does not matter for present purposes just how he assesses what is due to him, but it is simplest to assume that he accepts the evaluations embodied in the system and accepts or rejects his position in it according to whether or not, in his view, the authority got it right. He may, for example, believe that his efforts and achievements on behalf of the community should be recognized by the conferring of a knighthood.

The man who accepts his lowly position as what is due to him is the man who has humility, or the humble man.

Correspondingly, the man who accepts his noble position as what is due to him is the proud man. The two cases are quite parallel: as they both accept their respective position they perceive a 'fit' between it and their worth, and consequently do not here see any grounds for dissatisfaction. The perception of a fit precludes dissatisfaction with their positions. On the other hand, of course; the initial difference brings with it different behaviour and expectations: the humble will, for instance, expect to serve, the proud, conversely, to be served. Each man, given his clearly defined position in the system, will know what is expected of him and what in turn he can expect.

The position a man occupies in the hierarchical system need not remain static. The king may humble one or the other of his subjects by removing him from a relatively high position and putting him into a lower one, or he may elevate him to a higher one. So far the parallel holds. But there are complexities in the downward move which do not feature in that going in the opposite direction. The king may humiliate as well as humble. Humbling a person is the more neutral move, it consists simply in the downgrading of status for whatever reason. But intending to humiliate this person is in addition meant to show the world that he is worthy of less esteem than he had either been given or had assumed he deserved. So, for example, the penance at Canossa of Emperor Henry IV was a humiliation as well as a humbling. The Emperor was humbled by his visit to the Pope, for his taking such a step implied his acknowledgement that it was, after all, the Pope and not he who had the power to invest bishops in Germany. The visit itself therefore indicated that the Emperor had to accept a position which was less powerful than the one he had originally allotted to himself, and would have indicated this even if the Pope had graciously received him the moment he arrived. Instead, Pope Gregory kept him waiting on his doorstep for three days before admitting him to his presence. This was the humiliation. The Emperor's dignity was publicly lowered: everyone now knew that in not obeying the Pope as a Christian should, Henry had got above himself. He had to eat his words and deeds, he was put in his place.

Such objective humbling or humiliating need not be accompanied by a corresponding attitude on the part of him who suffered such a fate. Henry's visit to Gregory was not, as far as one can tell, undertaken in a humble spirit, and he seems to have regarded his humiliation as merely an event to be used to his political advantage. Where, however, a person does feel humbled this can be seen as the exact counterpart to the objective downward move. He feels humbled if, having previously regarded his higher position as the proper one, he now accepts the lower position as his due. He may think either that he had formerly taken an exaggerated view of his merits, or that, for some reason or other, his merits are now not what they once were. In either case, feeling humbled involves a downward revision of the agent's view of himself, parallel to the downgrading of his status. Feeling humiliated, on the other hand, does not imply the agent's acceptance of the new situation; his own view of himself and what is due to him may not change at all. But whether it does or not, he is aware that in the eyes of the world less is now due to him than was assumed or was formerly the case, and aware that to the eyes of the world he has been shown to have suffered from exaggerated self-esteem.

At the other end of the scale the position is somewhat different: while a person may of course be elevated as well as humbled, we have no analogous construction of 'pride' which can be used to describe the process of elevation, just as there is no contruction which can be used to mark the person's position in the system. To speak of a person as proud is always to refer to his attitude towards his position and so is to put him on a par with him who *feels* humble, or *feels* humiliated. The objective-subjective distinction does not here apply, nor does the process of elevating disclose two elements which can be compared with feeling humbled and feeling humiliated respectively. But there is a somewhat analogous distinction to be drawn here, viz., the distinction between the person who is proud, and the person who is proud of this or that. If we take the clue provided by the device of the hierarchical system then the person who is proud is one who recognizes his position as being relatively high and accepts it as his due[1]. But the person who is proud *of* his position does not think of it in these terms at all. In the following section I shall discuss in some detail this second type of pride before, in section 3, returning to the distinction between the two cases.

[1] This characterization does not fit all cases of pride. See text below, section 2.

2

Hume suggests that '*everything related to us, which produces pleasure or pain, produces likewise pride or humility*'.[2] In his view, pride is itself a feeling of pleasure which is parasitic on another feeling of pleasure derived from the perception or contemplation of some object which strikes the agent as agreeable in some respect. This initial pleasure is quite independent of the pleasure which is pride. I may just take pleasure in some beautiful house, say, and not feel proud at all. A further minimum condition to be fulfilled if I am to experience pride is that the beautiful house be in some way mine. This is how the self enters the analysis as part of what Hume calls the 'cause' of pride: whatever I am proud of must be 'related' to me. The self features again in the analysis as the 'object' of pride, as that towards which my pride is directed. So pride on this account can be summed up as consisting of a self-directed pleasure based on a distinct pleasure derived from something which is also mine.

I do not intend to discuss in detail Hume's analysis of pride as one of the indirect passions; his views on the distinction between 'cause' and 'object' of a passion and the mechanism of association have received a fair amount of attention.[3] I shall concentrate rather on only those points which bear directly on his explanation of the nature of pride. Here his major points are, I think, essentially correct. In particular, his distinction between the cause and the obejct of pride indicates the fundamental structure of the emotion.[4] But what he wants to say can be put in less misleading terminology. Restating his insights in terms of explanatory and identificatory beliefs will reveal more clearly what pride consists in, and will also sort out the ambiguities in some of Hume's assertions.

Hume is not entirely satisfied with his account of pride as it stands. The problem that worries him is that it is just not the

[2] *A Treatise of Human Nature*, ed. L. A. Selby-Bigge (Clarendon Press, 1967), Book 2, Part 1, section VI. p. 291. (All following page references will be to this edition.)

[3] See for example Páll S. Árdall, *Passion and Value in Hume's Treatise* (Edinburgh University Press, 1966); and Jerome Neu, *Emotion, Thought and Therapy* (Routledge and Kegan Paul, 1978).

[4] For a sympathetic discussion see Annette Baier's paper 'Hume's Analysis of Pride', *Journal of Philosophy*, Vol. lxxv, No. 1 (January 1978).

case that everything that is related to us and produces pleasure also produces pride. The agent may continue to feel joy or pleasure in this self-related agreeable object and fail to make the transition to the second, self-directed pleasure which is pride. So, Hume thinks, we have to impose certain limitations on the relation between the self and that agreeable object, as well as on the object itself as a source of pleasure. The relation must be a 'close' one, and the agreeable object comparatively rare, fairly constant, and discernible to others as well as to the agent himself. So the problem he quite properly sets himself to solve is how pride is to be distinguished from other, similar emotions. His framework of various feelings tied together by association allowed him to speak of the relevant conditions as merely holding 'normally' when some agent experiences pride; but given their function of individuating pride and separating it from other passions they quite naturally present themselves as candidates for a set of necessary conditions which must obtain if a person is to feel pride.

The most important requirement for pride, but not for joy or pleasure, is that the relation between the self and the agreeable object be a 'close' one. The only clarification Hume offers of what a 'close' relation might consist in appears in the form of an example, and there it is hinted at rather than spelt out. His point is that joy is based on a 'slighter' relation than pride and vainglory:

We may feel joy upon being present at a feast, where our senses are regal'd with delicacies of every kind: But 'tis only the master of the feast, who, beside the same joy, has the additional passion of self-applause and vanity. (290.)

So while a guest may feel joy or pleasure on the basis of being present at a feast, only the master, who organized it, can feel proud of it. 'Being present at' is not a close enough relation for the purpose. This sounds as if Hume is suggesting that it is possible to enumerate different relations and to pronounce each as close or not close enough for pride, as the case may be. But it turns out that this is not quite what he has in mind, for he immediately produces a counter-example. It is quite possible, he admits, that men by so 'small' a relation as 'being present at' convert their pleasure into pride, and 'boast of a great entertainment, at which they have only been present' (290). The suggestion here is that someone sufficiently determined to shine can somehow build his pride on a relation which is not really adequate. Hume, it is clear, regards such people as uncommonly silly and so perhaps as not requiring serious attention, for he concludes: 'this must in general be own'd, that joy arises from a more inconsiderable relation than vanity, and that many things, which are too foreign to produce pride, are yet able to give us a delight and pleasure.' (290-1.)

If we are looking for a feature which will enable us to distinguish pride from joy or pleasure then this account of the requisite type of connection has failed to provide it. The boastful guest is allowed to be proud of the feast in spite of it being only 'slightly' related to him, though we are meant to infer that he is not at all sensible in being proud, that he has no reason for his pride. But if a relation like 'being present at' will do for pride which is not rational then the condition that the connection be a close one would seem to distinguish not pride from joy and pleasure, but distinguish at best rational from irrational pride.

Hume confuses the issue by running together two distinguishable cases. In both of them the relation between the guest and the feast is 'being present at'. It is given that he is just present at the feast. But whether or not this relation can be a basis for any sort of pride depends not on the guest's actual circumstances, but depends on the beliefs he holds about his circumstances; given these, the case of the boastful guest can be disentangled. He may believe, and say so in explanation of his pride, that he was just present at the feast. This might make his claim intelligible if it turns out that what he is proud of is the *success* of the feast, and that he also believes that he was the life and soul of the party; or perhaps that his distinction and fame are such that his mere presence is sufficient to turn every function he attends into a success. But Hume's example suggests rather that it is not its success but the *occurrence* of the feast that is in question. The master without whose efforts it would not have taken place at all can be proud of its occurrence. The guest's claim that he is proud of the occurrence of the feast is either unintelligible or irrational. It is unintelligible if he insists that his mere presence is his sole reason for being proud of the feast; in that case we should be inclined to say that whatever his feelings on this occasion may be, they cannot be feelings of pride. It is irrational if it turns out that in the face of overwhelming evidence the guest has managed to persuade himself that somehow he had a hand in bringing the feast about. In that case it may be pride he is feeling, but he has no rational basis for his pride. Hume, in ignoring the guest's beliefs, switches from one case to the other, and so blurs the distinction.

Hume is wrong, then, in setting out the conditions of pride in the way he does: they cannot be stated in terms of what is as a matter of fact the case, but must be stated in terms of the beliefs of the person concerned. The introduction of beliefs gives the Humean points a new framework which will put right what he has got wrong, while still preserving his considerable insights. Within the new framework his 'causes' become explanatory beliefs, and what they explain is the person's identificatory belief, that which identifies the feeling as pride rather than some other emotion. It is this latter belief which has to accommodate the crucial feature of pride, that it is reflexive. Hume expressed this point by saying that the 'object' of pride is self. But the object terminology is unfortunate.[5] If we take it, as Hume seems to have done, that 'object' means 'object of attention' or 'that which the person's interest is directed towards', then what he says is just not true: the object of pride in this sense may or may not be the self. Often it is rather what is referred to by the phrase completing the expression 'he is proud of ....', which for Hume is the *cause* and not the *object* of pride. On those occasions when I am proud of myself it is the self which is the object, but when feeling proud of my house, my car, or my children my attention is more likely to be directed towards them and not towards myself. Nevertheless, it is because a view of myself is in some way involved that my feeling is pride and not just pleasure in their respective qualities. My mode of attention is of a specific kind, for I look at them from the point of view of how their desirable qualities reflect on my own standing. In being proud of my house, car, or children I think well of not just them; I think well also of myself just

[5] Neu argues that for Hume's theory of association it is a disaster. See Neu, *Emotion, Thought and Therapy*, Part 1, sections 7–9.

because I can think well of them. Through my possession of or relation to them my own standing, I think, is also now improved.

This crucial feature of pride, its reference to self, is taken care of by formulating it in terms of the agent's identificatory belief. The phrasing of this belief will vary somewhat, depending on whether pride is taken to be occurrent or dispositional. If the latter, then the person concerned will believe that in a certain respect (as house-owner, parent, etc.) she is of worth. But if the emotion is thought of as occurrent then the upheaval of an emotional experience has to be reflected in the identificatory belief: at the time of its occurrence the person feeling pride believes that in a certain respect her own worth is confirmed or enhanced. In pride the 'upheaval' is likely to be a mild one, but there is at the moment of feeling it an awareness that she has reason to think well of herself, and so at least at that moment she takes a different view of herself. It may be different only in that she had before that moment not been thinking about herself at all; or it may be different in that she now thinks better of herself than she did before. In experiencing the emotion she experiences a boost to her self-esteem or her self-confidence; otherwise it would not be pride she would be feeling. I can think well of and take pleasure in all sorts of possessions or relations of mine without being proud of them. In that case the value I see in them remains 'external' to me: for some reason or other I cannot, or anyway do not, use it to improve my view of myself.

Given that this is the kind of identificatory belief we need, what sorts of explanatory beliefs should we look for? The function of these beliefs is to explain in virtue of what I believe my worth to be confirmed or enhanced. In Hume's terminology, we are looking for the causes of pride, and if we follow his lead then this feeling is explained by the reference to the pleasure I derive from the thing in question, together with my belief that this thing is in some way connected with me. The second condition is correct, but needs elucidation. The condition that I must derive pleasure from that thing is, however, unacceptable. 'Taking pleasure in' or 'being pleased by' is too weak a reaction to account for a person's increased self-esteem or self-confidence. We prize or value what we are proud of, and this is

different from, and may not coincide with, finding it pleasant.[6]
I may value something, or think it desirable, without deriving
pleasure from it or be pleased by it but not value it at all. I may
even take pleasure in some possession of mine and feel ashamed
rather than proud of it. So an appeal to pleasure will not do as
an explanatory move. To think well of himself the person feeling proud must also think well of, i.e., value, that which he is
proud of. Expressed in terms of an explanatory belief the condition therefore reads: if a person is proud of something then he
believes that thing to be of value. He will of course value it
under some description, and it is the reference to what he
values under the relevant description which will explain his
pride. The master of the feast who is proud of its success may,
as it happens, not set much store by successful feasts as such.
But in that case he will value some other features of the situation, a duty well performed, perhaps, or his ability as an
organizer.

Hume introduces two conditions, expressed as limitations to
the causes of pride, which are relevant to the explanatory belief
under discussion. He thinks that what we are proud of must be
discernible and obvious to others:

the third limitation is, that the pleasant . . . object be very discernible
and obvious, and that not only to ourselves, but to others also. This
circumstance . . . has an effect upon joy, as well as pride. We fancy
ourselves more happy, as well as more virtuous or beautiful, when we
appear so to others; but are still more ostentatious of our virtues than
of our pleasures. (292.)

He further points out that general rules have a strong influence
on pride:

as custom and practice have brought to light all these principles, and
have settled the value of everything; this must certainly contribute to
the easy production of the passions, and guide us, by means of
general establish'd maxims, in the proportion we ought to observe in
preferring one object to another. (294.)

The point Hume seems to be making here is that there is a
strong conventional element in pride, but the respect in which

---

[6] This point is of course unacceptable to someone who, like Hume, analyses valuing
itself in terms of pleasure. But this is just wrong. For some remarks on what it is to
value something see Ch. V.

it is conventional is different in the two limitations. The second point, that general rules influence what we think of value, and to what degree, suggests no more than that our value-judgements are not formed independently of the rules and conventions of the society in which we live; a point which can hardly be disputed. But that what we are proud of be discernible and obvious to others makes a quite different point, namely that what we are proud of should be an object of approval also to others, and this is a rather more dubious proposition. If the implication is that we are proud of qualities etc. only in so far as they are likely to gain the admiration and approval of society then this is probably empirically false, and is in any case not necessarily so.[7] Naturally, we like to be approved of and admired, but this is not sufficient to limit what we can be proud of. As I shall explain later, we may be proud of something we have, or have done, and feel shame or humiliation at being proud of such a thing.[8] In that case the last thing we are likely to want is for the 'cause' of our pride to be obvious to others. All one can extract from Hume's limitation is that in many or perhaps 'normal' cases of pride what the person is proud of he will regard as something others value, too, and would be proud to possess or have done.

But Hume's remark may after all point to a general truth about pride: it may be that there are limits to what we can be proud of because there are limits to what we can value. Whether this is so or not depends on what is to be understood by valuing something, a point to which I shall return later (Ch. V). It is at least plausible to suggest that to value something is to see it as either a (human) good or as the means towards achieving such a good. This does not mean that a person can value only what is conventionally so regarded. She may think herself, and perhaps be, more perceptive or less

[7] For a discussion of this point see Arnold Isenberg 'Natural Pride and Natural Shame' in *Explaining Emotions*, ed. Amélie Oksenberg Rorty. I interpret Hume here illegitimately as making conceptual points about the nature of pride. This is not of course his approach. But as my interest is not primarily in Hume's system I feel justified in interpreting his remarks in the way in which they can best serve to illuminate important features of pride.

[8] Of course a person cannot at the same time be proud and ashamed of one and the same thing, under the same description, as he could take pleasure in and be ashamed of it at the same time. The object of his shame in the present case is not what he is proud of, but is the fact that he is proud of it.

prejudiced than others and so see value where others do not. Of course, unless she can make her position clear to others her pride will remain unintelligible to them, but it may be pride she is feeling nevertheless. The restriction is not that she cannot be proud of this or that because others do not see its value. The restriction is rather that she must believe that if only others were more intelligent or less trivially minded they, too, would come to value that thing, or at least come to see that it might be valued. If she did not hold that belief she could not be said to value the thing in question. If this is so then the correct version of Hume's limitation on the cause of pride is not that the value of what a person is proud of must be plain to all; it is that the person must think her view of what is valuable in the situation is one that can at least in principle be shared with others. And this limitation is implied by the condition that if a person is to be proud of something she must believe it to be of value. Pride is not 'conventional' in the sense that what I am proud of must be an object of approval to others; I need not even think that this is the case. Hume is right to introduce a reference to others, but it is not in a straightforward way that they or their approval are required. But this is not to deny, of course, that we are much more likely to be proud of what is conventionally thought worth having than of something whose value we take to be hidden from others, nor is it to deny that sometimes we are proud of something because we know it to be admired by others, rather than particularly valued by ourselves.

What I am proud of I must see as capable of boosting my self-esteem or as confirming my confidence in myself. For it to play that role I must indeed believe it to be in some way connected with me. Hume correctly pointed out the oddity of claiming to be proud of the beautiful fish in the ocean, or an animal in the desert (303). For me to be proud of something I must regard it as my such-and-such, or as my so-and-so's such-and-such, but the ocean or the desert are not mine, nor did I have a hand in the creation of the beautiful fish or the animal. But a person may, crazily, believe that he did. The condition for a person feeling pride is not that the object in question be connected with him, but only that he believe this to be the case. But given this, the point that the person must see himself connected with what he is proud of still needs elucidation. Maybe it can be restated as a point of grammar and read: 'whatever expression completes the sense of the verb ". . . is proud of . . ." must begin with "his own".'[9] Hume's requirement that the connection be a close one can then be taken as the point that the relation which the person believes to hold between himself and the relevant thing or event must be such that it makes sense for him to speak of *his* so-and-so. Clearly, not all relations allow this further step; the person claiming to be proud of the fish in the ocean would remain unintelligible if he insisted that the only relation holding between him and it was that of observer to thing observed. If this is all Hume had in mind when stipulating that the connection be a close one, then the condition incorporating his point reads: only what a person can intelligibly speak of as his so-and-so is a possible object of pride for him. This is true, and it is a condition which applies to pride but not to joy or pleasure, for what gives pleasure need not in this way be connected with the person concerned.

It is also a condition which would support the only partially formulated claim of Hume's, viz., that some relations are too 'slight' to allow the further step of regarding as his whatever he, in his own view, is related to in this manner. Seeing the relation between himself and the fish as that of observer to observed he is not on that basis alone entitled to speak of *his* fish, and similarly, seeing the relation between himself and the feast as that of being present at, he cannot in virtue of just that relation refer to the feast as his. We can, then, characterize a 'slight' relation as one which does not permit the move of regarding the thing in question as his. Of course, what turns out to be a 'slight' relation in one set of circumstances may not be so in another; being present at the feast may be enough for the guest to speak of his success. It is, however, not clear that whatever relation by this criterion does not turn out to be 'slight', is therefore a 'close' one. What remains unexplained, and what, I think, Hume was also concerned with when he stipulated that the connection be 'close', is that of all the enormous number of diverse relations which may hold between a person and some other person(s) or thing and which do entitle

---

[9] This is Anthony Kenny's formulation in *Action, Emotion and the Will* (Routledge and Kegan Paul, 1963), p. 23. (Kenny proposes this formulation as making Hume's point that one is always proud of oneself. But this misinterprets Hume.)

him to speak of 'my . . . . ', only a few are immediately acceptable as a basis of pride. The expression '. . . is proud of . . .'
may be completed by 'my neighbour', 'my predecessor', etc.,
but this relation by itself is not 'close' enough to explain his
pride. It is only if the blank is filled by the description of a personal quality, a possession, or something he has brought about,
that no further explanation seems to be required. This suggests
a more substantial version of the condition that a person must
be closely connected with what he is proud of: what a person is
proud of he must regard as something he owns or as something
for the existence of which he is responsible. The connection
between the person experiencing pride and what he is proud of
would then be 'close' simply in that what he is proud of is seen
by him as his possession or his creation.

This suggestion implies that although I can speak of, for
example, my country or my grandfather without thinking of
them as my possessions or creations, I must think of them in
just these terms if I am to be proud of them. In some cases this
seems more plausible than in others. A parent may see his son
as his possession and his cleverness as that quality in virtue of
which he is proud of this possession of his. This would make
being proud of his clever son exactly similar to his being proud
of the beautiful house he owns. Alternatively, he may think of
his clever son as his creation, on the grounds perhaps that the
son's cleverness is an inheritance from him, or because he
created conditions in which such cleverness could flourish. This
would be parallel to his being proud of the beautiful house not
on the grounds of just ownership but because he has made it
beautiful. He is the architect, the builder or decorator. In this
case he would be proud of his son's cleverness or the beauty of
the house, rather than proud of a possession in virtue of that
possession having a desirable quality. The expression 'I am
proud of my clever son (beautiful house)' does not make it clear
which of these alternatives applies, while 'I am proud of my
son's cleverness' implies the second and not the first of the two
possibilities.

It is of course much more strange to think of one's grandfather (neighbour, friend, compatriot) as one's possession, let
alone think of one's clever grandfather as one's creation, than
it is to think in these terms one's son. But to be proud of an

ancestor is an acceptable and quite common case of pride, and
so it is unlikely that such far-fetched beliefs must be assumed.
The suggested formulation of the necessary condition for pride
in terms of possession improves on the grammatical one in that
it is more explanatory, but it errs in introducing too much content. It is just not true that I cannot be proud of my son, friend
or grandfather unless I regard them as possessions of mine; the
relation need not be as 'close' as all that. Nor can it be as simply
characterized. It is, in general, the relation of belonging. It is in
virtue of belonging to the same family, the same country or
institution that people are proud of their ancestors, country-
men, or colleagues. The belonging may be quite straightforward, as it is between me and my house. Or it may hold the
other way about: my belonging to a nation or institution makes
that nation or institution and its belongings a possible object of
pride for me. Or again, in belonging to some country or institution, others who also belong to that country or institution
may present themselves as something to be proud of. The relation of belonging operates in various directions and all of them
can be exploited from the point of view of feeling proud. It can
be the basis for pride in quite different ways: I may, but need
not think of my son or grandfather as my belongings in order to
be proud of them, nor need I think of their desirable qualities
as something I have helped to bring about in order to be proud
of these. I need not, for example, regard my grandfather's wit
as something I am at least partially responsible for; rather more
sanely, I may see him as sharing with me the relation of 'belonging to the same family'. This allows me to identify with him as
a member of that family and see his belongings as something
in which I have a share and so can be proud of. On similar
bases I may be proud of my son's cleverness, my father's riches,
or my country's prosperity. The bonds of nationality or family
allow such identifications. It would seem indeed that family or
tribal or national bonds, i.e., those created by circumstances of
birth, are thought to be of more fundamental significance to the
person concerned than are those that have come his way or
have been brought about by him in the course of his life. They
seem to be given a privileged position in that they and only they
seem to allow the move from 'I am proud of so-and-so' to 'I am
proud of so-and-so's belonging'. At least, a person's claim that

he is proud of his grandfather's wit seems more acceptable than the claim that he is proud of the wit of someone with whom he shares the same profession (political party, school, etc.). Although I may be proud of my predecessor on the basis of belonging to the same profession, or more narrowly, on the basis of belonging to the set of members of that profession who held the same post, it is not so clear that I can therefore be proud of her wit. The bond is not deemed close enough to allow of identification. If this is so then there is here a conventional constraint on what a person may be proud of.[10] But it may not be so. It is perhaps unlikely that it should always be possible to tell whether some unusual claim fails to meet the conditions for feeling proud altogether, or whether it is a case of quite irrational pride. Perhaps the claim to be proud of one's predecessor's wit falls into the second category.

It is of course a fact about a person that he belongs to this family, that country or profession, and it may be a fact to which he pays little or no attention. But if he is proud of his grandfather, his local football team, or his predecessor then it must be a fact that weighs with him. He must think that it is true of the persons he is proud of that they stand in the relation of belonging to him, in one or another of its possible forms, and it is with this in mind that he assesses their respective qualities. The formulation in terms of belonging therefore adds content to, and so is more explanatory than, the initial grammatical formulation. I may not think of my compatriot, neighbour or friend as belonging to me in any way and thus omit to take the step which would turn them into possible objects of pride. On the other hand, I cannot regard them as belongings of mine at all if I cannot refer to them as 'my so-and-so'. The grammatical requirement is presupposed by the present one and need no longer be spelt out specifically as one of the conditions of pride.

---

[10] It is not quite true that only bonds created by circumstances of birth are given privileged status: we may be proud of the belongings of a grandfather we have acquired through adoption rather than birth, or of a country whose citizen we have chosen to become. We may also be proud of the belongings of a husband or wife. The thought that husband and wife are really one will no doubt account for the latter case, in spite of the changing views of the nature of marriage. And the first case may support rather than contradict the point made in the text: the significance conventionally attributed to country or family as one's origins is so great that it can carry over to cases where country and family do not in fact mark one's origins.

I am grateful to Nancy Davis for suggesting the cases discussed in this connection.

The formulation in terms of belonging has also the advantage of not introducing too much content, as did the one in terms of ownership or possession. 'Belonging to' is a weaker relation than that of ownership, in that it does not imply, as ownership does, that the person concerned has any particular rights concerning the use or disposal of whatever he is so related to. Possession becomes merely a special case of belonging, as being a belonging with regard to which the person concerned has certain rights, so that cases where what that person is proud of is regarded by him as a possession are covered by the suggested relation.

The proposed necessary conditions for feeling pride now read: if a person feels proud of something then he must believe this thing (person) to be in some respect desirable or valuable, and he must believe that the relation of belonging in one of its various forms holds between him and it (him, her). We can add to the second requirement: or he must believe that he is at least partially responsible for bringing it about. Alternatively, for the sake of neatness and economy, we may treat the case of 'being responsible for' as falling under the relation of belonging: where an agent is proud of something he has brought about, that which he has brought about would then be regarded as an event which 'belongs' to the agent in the sense that he is at least partially responsible for its existence. We may treat similarly the case where a person is proud not of something he has or has done, but is proud of standing in a certain relationship to a thing or person. He is proud not of his beautiful house, but is proud of owning a house (any old house). 'Owning a house' is now what he sees as desirable and as 'belonging' to him. It may belong to him in the sense that it is a state he is responsible for having brought about. But ownership of that house may have fallen into his lap without any effort on his part. Then the ownership is a belonging of his in much the same way as his personal characteristics, his handsome face or his sense of humour, may be said to be belongings of his.

The new formulation suggests another interpretation of what might be a relation which is 'too slight' a basis for pride: very many quite different relations allow a person to speak of 'my so-and-so', but by no means all of these involve the relation of belonging in any of the various acceptable ways. I can, for example, speak of my taxi-driver. Conceivably, I may be proud of him if, say, he acts with great presence of mind in an emergency. Then I see him as in some way belonging to me. The basis for seeing him in this way is slight indeed; a person would have to be very anxious to acquire reflected glory if she is proud of somebody to whom she is connected in just this way. So this may be a case where I (foolishly, unreasonably) turn a very slight relation into one which is suitable for pride. A close connection, on this interpretation, would then be one which can be properly expressed in terms of belonging, so that my believing this relation to exist between myself and what I am proud of is supported by what is as a matter of fact the case. The two interpretations of 'slight' connection do, of course, correspond to the different kinds of failure which I accused Hume of not disentangling. On the first interpretation a slight connection between a person and some other thing was one which did not permit that person to speak of the thing as 'his', just on the basis of that relation. The fish I observe is not therefore my fish, and the feast I am present at is not therefore my feast. My claim to be proud of the fish or the feast would therefore be unintelligible; whatever my feelings may be, they cannot be pride. This is so, at any rate, unless by assuming the agent to hold irrational beliefs about his powers we can make some sense of his regarding these things as his. On the present characterization of 'slight connexion' pride may be experienced on the basis of it, for the relation between the person concerned and what he claims to be proud of is such that he can properly refer to it as his. But it would be unreasonable pride because there seems no good reason why, given the connection, the agent should now think more of himself. Hume wanted it to be possible for a person to turn a slight connection into the close one required for pride. This is more plausible on the second interpretation: that person would then be foolish as he has very little grounds for his increased self-esteem. It is an unreasonable but nevertheless perfectly normal and possibly even common occurrence of pride. On the first interpretation, on the other hand, the person bent on turning a slight relation into a close one would have to collect a set of wholly irrational beliefs in order to count as being proud at all, and this is a highly implausible suggestion.

So far I have tried to elucidate what in Hume's terminology were the 'causes' of pride, and to reformulate these in terms of explanatory beliefs. It is the role of these beliefs to explain the identificatory belief, and it is because they have this role that they are what they are, that is, refer to something 'closely' related to the person in question. It is also because they have this role that they can be judged to be adequate or otherwise. Certain relations are implausible and far-fetched as a basis of pride and throw no light on why a person's standing or worth should be affected one way or another by his standing in this relation to whatever he is proud of, and the corresponding belief would therefore not adequately explain his state. My relation to the taxi-driver, for example, is too casual, too fleeting, and too arbitrary to be sensibly thought of as having this effect.[11]

The explanatory beliefs explain, but do not entail the identificatory belief. A person may hold the requisite explanatory beliefs and yet not feel proud: we cannot infer from the fact that she regards something or other as a valuable belonging of hers that she is therefore proud of it. She may regard her beautiful house as a most desirable possession but may not regard this as reflecting on her own worth. This option is open even where she regards the desirable as something she herself has brought about. She may have been promoted and now occupy a higher position in the office's hierarchy. She may think the promotion due to her ability and devotion to duty, so that to some extent the occupation of the higher position is, in her view, her own doing. She may also think that it has all sorts of desirable features, such as financial and social advantages, more interesting work, and so on. So she values occupying the higher position. But holding all these beliefs her thoughts about her own worth may not thereby be affected. They will be so only if she also values her occupying the higher position. That is to say, to state conditions which are sufficient for pride and not merely necessary requires reference to the self in the spelling out of what the person values: she must value not just whatever she thinks of as standing in the relation of belonging to her, but

---

[11] This is the truth contained in Hume's fourth limitation: 'It seems ridiculous to infer an excellency in ourselves from an object, which is of so much shorter duration, and attends us during so small a part of our existence.' (p. 293.)

must value also her standing in that relation to the thing or person in question.

A person experiencing pride values, for example, her beautiful house; because she does so, she values her ownership of the house. But if she values her ownership of the house then she values her being the owner of it, and so values herself-as-its-owner. Her standing in the given relation to the house provides the link with the self, and her belief about the worth of the relation provides the link with her belief about the worth of that self. The valuing of her ownership is what Hume refers to as that pleasure which is pride. It is indeed different from the valuing of the house, or from valuing ownership of it, since it has a different object, and need not be its consequence. It follows that this final belief, that what is of value is the person's standing in the relationship of belonging to the thing in question, is related to the identificatory belief in a way which is different from that in which the explanatory beliefs discussed earlier are related to it. These gave her reasons for her pride, they explained but did not entail her identificatory belief, that (in a certain respect) she is of worth, or that her worth in this respect is confirmed or enhanced. The present belief is also not entailed by the explanatory beliefs, but, like the identificatory one, is causally dependent on them. It expresses the shift in the direction of her thoughts, from the belief concerning some thing or other person, some action or state, to a belief concerning herself. Because the house is a splendid belonging of hers, its belonging to her, too, is a splendid thing, and so finally, is she to whom it belongs, i.e. she who has the property of owning that fine house.[12]

3

A person may be proud of many things, including himself.[13] But he may also be just proud, and not be proud of this or that. How are these two types of pride related to each other?

[12] Cp. Baier, 'Hume's Analysis of Pride', p. 29 ff. It is true, therefore, that, as she points out, Davidson's suggestion that her being proud of something reduces to her being proud that . . . ignores the complexity of pride, for it fails to separate the two items which Hume properly distinguished: the pleasure which is pride, and the pleasure taken in what she is proud of.

[13] Not in the sense in which, ultimately, pride is always self-directed, but in the

Hume sometimes seems to assume that here we do not have two sorts of cases, but that to explain the one is also to explain the other. This view is suggested by a number of his remarks. So, for example, he takes himself to be arguing against traditional doctrine when he claims that 'consider'd in themselves' pride is by no means always vicious nor humility always virtuous.[14] But what is traditionally regarded as vicious is pride the character-trait rather than pride the passion. It is at least not obviously the case that a person who is proud of many of his deeds and characteristics is the person who has this trait; on the contrary, it seems quite possible for him frequently to experience pride (in himself) and yet to remain quite humble. Again, he may possess the virtue of humility and yet not be prone to suffer frequently the unpleasant experience of self-dissatisfaction, which for Hume constitutes the passion of humility. So if Hume thinks of himself as breaking with tradition in claiming that pride may not be vicious, he must be thinking of the character-trait; but as this view forms part of his lengthy discussion of pride the passion the implication seems to be that he takes the proud man to be identical with the man who is proud of himself. But this is a mistake.

In an earlier section I characterized the person who is proud as accepting his high position as his due. But this description does not fit the person who is proud *of* his position. The contrast is well illustrated by the respective attitudes to their position of the Jane Austen characters, Sir William Lucas and Mr. Darcy. Sir William had 'risen to the honour of knighthood by an address to the king, during his mayoralty'.[15] He is inordinately proud of his new status. 'The distinction had perhaps

sense that the explanatory beliefs make reference to a characteristic or doing of the agent himself.

[14] 2.1.VII (297). In his account of the correspondence of passions in men and animals Hume sometimes seems to refer to the characteristic pride as expressed in a certain type of behaviour, and sometimes to what may be taken to be pride the passion: 'The very port and gait of a swan, or turkey, or peacock show the high idea he has entertain'd of himself, and his contempt of all others.' (326) But: 'The vanity and emulation of nightingales in singing have been commonly remark'd; as likewise that of horses in swiftness, of hounds in sagacity and smell, of the bull and cock in strength, and of every other animal in his particular excellency.' The nightingale, the horse, the hound, bull and cock seem to be proud of their gift; the swan, turkey and peacock are simply proud.

[15] All the references are to Chapter V of *Pride and Prejudice*.

been felt too strongly', Jane Austen remarks. But he is not a proud man. What is distinctive about his case is that he gives a great deal of thought to his knighthood, to the difference it has made and, he thinks, should make to his standing and behaviour. It had, for instance, 'given him a disgust to his business, and to his residence in a small market town'. This attitude can be contrasted with that of Mr. Darcy, owner of Pemberley and with an income of £10,000 a year. Mr. Darcy is a proud man, but he is not proud of his high position on the social scale. Unlike Sir William he does not think of his position as somehow adding to his importance and worth, for he takes it totally for granted. The description of the proud man as accepting his high position as his due does not imply that he must have assessed his position and his 'inner worth' independently of each other and then discovered that they matched; he may not think of his social position as reflecting his worth, but think of it rather as partially constituting it. This is the case with Mr. Darcy. His social standing is, in his view, intimately connected with his general standing: intellectually and morally he is superior to others as well, and the superiorities are interconnected. Unlike Sir William he need not and does not give a thought to his status: seeing his worth in the terms he does rules it out that he should think of his social position as enhancing him, for it is part of a whole already perfect. While he feels secure in this belief he need not think about his standing at all; not that he does not value it, but he is accustomed to taking it as a matter of course.

Mr. Darcy was born into his position, Sir William had his thrust upon him. But this is not the crux of the matter, though it of course helps to explain why the two men have the attitudes they have. But men of Darcy's standing in society may well be proud of it, while a different Sir William might take his elevation in his stride. It is the nature of their attitudes itself which is of crucial importance. Mr. Darcy shares Sir William's view that a relatively high position on the scale is of great value, and in his case, too, this belief permeates his life and is responsible for much of what he does and thinks. But in his life the role allotted to the belief is different from the one it plays in Sir William's.

The difference between the two cases lies in the different expectations of the people involved. Sir William's self-esteem is boosted by his elevation to a higher status. But it would not have had that effect on him if being given this kind of distinction had been just something he took for granted, if he had regarded it as a matter of course that he was the sort of man whose services would deservedly be recognized in this way. It is this feature which characterizes the case of the person who experiences pride the passion and distinguishes it from that of pride the character-trait. What a person is proud of in some way exceeds what in his own view he can expect as a matter of course. If he regards certain activities, possessions, or alignments of his as the norm of what he can expect, then to be proud of some deed or possession he must see it as being beyond this norm. Put more economically, what a person is proud of he sees as an achievement of his. 'Achievement' in this context does not have the usual implication that if a person has achieved something then he has made an effort to bring it about; it is rather to be understood in this minimal sense, that a person has achieved something if possession of that thing, or belonging to it, or having brought it about, goes beyond what in his own view he could expect.

What a person is proud of is to him an achievement in that it goes beyond his norm of expectations. How this norm is arrived at (and of course it will not remain static) depends on very many sorts of factors. It will depend partly on the social and economic conditions of the time and place. So anything that is rare and therefore hard to come by will for that reason be beyond the ordinary person's norm of expectations and so be a possible object of pride for him. This is the kernel of truth in a suggestion of Hume's concerning a constraint on the causes of pride which has not yet been mentioned. He tells us that what we are proud of is restricted to what is comparatively rare:

We are rejoyc'd for many goods, which, on account of their frequency, give us no pride. Health, when it returns after a long absence, affords us a very sensible satisfaction; but it is seldom regarded as a subject of vanity, because 'tis shar'd with such vast numbers. (292.)

But I may be proud of my health, and these days people quite often are. The reason for this may, however, be a Humean one: what is frequent or rare may not be so absolutely but may depend on a society's social and economic conditions, so that what on these grounds may be a possible object of pride for one society, or for one section of it, may not be so for another. We are constantly told, as Hume presumably was not, that health is hard to come by and needs much effort and care to keep. But this does not go to the heart of the matter; it is not really the widespread distribution of the good or the frequency or otherwise of its occurrence which is here at stake. It is again the agent's view that matters: maybe normal people in normal circumstances take health for granted and are not proud of their possession of it. But I or my circumstances may not be normal and I may be proud of my health, and for this to be the case it is quite irrelevant how many normal people there are about. It may be that keeping my health costs me more effort than is normal and so I am proud of it in that possession of it goes beyond what I can take for granted. Or it may be that I consider myself to be generally below what I take to be normal and so am proud of any possession that puts me in the group of 'normal people'. Hume ignored the agent's view of the situation, and so mistook for a general constraint what is merely a possible instance of it: the crux of the matter is not how rarely or frequently the relevant goods are to be met with as a matter of fact, but how rare or common they are in relation to the particular agent, in that agent's own view. One reason, but one reason only, why possession of some things may be beyond what he can expect is that such things are, as it happens, so rare. But it is quite possible that he regards some good, however widely distributed it may be, as not at all easily within his grasp. If this is the basis from which he starts then he may well feel proud if after all he finds himself in possession of such a good.

An agent's norm of expectations, what he does or does not at certain periods of his life think he can take for granted, does not, then, depend solely on external circumstances, it also depends on what in his view he should make of his life, and on his view of his capacities for achieving what he thinks worthwhile. His view of what he can or cannot do, of what situations he can or cannot cope with, will determine his normal expectations in this respect. So his degree of self-confidence will be an important factor in settling what he is or is not proud of. Where expectations are pitched low the occasions for thinking of oneself as having achieved something are particularly numerous. If I think of myself as the sort of person who cannot make machines work for them or whose flowers die on them, then any successful operation of the machine and any flourishing of my plants will be seen as an achievement and so as something to be proud of. But one need not start with a pessimistic view of oneself to find plenty of occasions for collecting achievements. Maybe the master of the feast who lacks confidence in his ability to organize feasts is more likely to be proud of its success than is that master who takes it as a matter of course that any feast he organizes will be successful. But this second master may still be proud of the feast's success. If so, then it is not in relation to his own abilities that he sees it as an achievement; rather, the success is beyond his norm of expectations because there are, in his view, so few efficient organizers of feasts that success just cannot be taken for granted. It is in relation to what, things being what they are, can be expected of masters of feasts that he thinks he shines, and that the successful feast can be taken by him as a boost to his self-esteem. There are at least three different ways in which a norm of expectation may be established: a norm is given by what a person thinks he can expect as a matter of course in relation to external circumstances, such as the rarity or frequency of the thing or his financial and social circumstances. A norm is also given by his view of his own abilities and limitations, by what he thinks he can or cannot do. And finally, a norm is given by the person's view of the expectations of others, by what in his view society expects or can expect in this or that area of life.

It is then, in a variety of ways and from a variety of points of view that what a person is proud of goes beyond that person's norm of expectations, and in whatever way she sees it as exceeding what she thinks she can expect, she will see it as an achievement of hers. So there seems to be here another belief required of the person who is proud of something, viz., that she sees what she is connected with and thinks desirable as such an achievement. But this would be a mistaken formulation of such a belief. For while it is her beautiful house which she believes to be a valuable possession of hers, it is not the beautiful house which she regards as the achievement; the achievement is her ownership of it, or her having built it or painted it, or whatever. That is, what in all cases of pride is seen as an achievement is not the desirable belonging, but is that she should be connected with it in the way she is. In the last section I pointed out that a person may value some possession and yet not be proud of it; to feel pride she must value also her possessing it. And it is precisely what she must also value that she will see as an achievement. The notion of achievement clarifies the respect in which she values the connection: she values it in that she sees it as being beyond her norm of expectations in the sense of it being better than for some reason or another she thinks she is, or others are, entitled to expect.

This completes the analysis of pride the passion: a person who experiences pride believes that she stands in the relation of belonging to some object (person, deed, state) which she thinks desirable in some respect. This is the general description of the explanatory beliefs. It is because (in her view) this relation holds between her and the desirable object that she believes her worth to be increased, in the relevant respect. This belief is constitutive of the feeling of pride. The gap between the explanatory and identificatory beliefs is bridged by the belief that her connection to the thing in question is itself of value, or is an achievement of hers.

The introduction of the final belief suggests a third interpretation of what might be meant by the 'close connexion' Hume speaks of. On this interpretation a person is closely connected to, for instance, the beautiful house if he sees its belonging to him as an achievement. This would give the close connection a different status from the one suggested earlier. It would become constitutive of feeling proud. For the requirement now states that, to be an object of pride, the desirable belonging has to be seen from a certain point of view, as a candidate for playing a certain kind of role in the person's self-related expectations. Otherwise, however much he values this possession, it will not become an object of pride. Therefore, as a possible object for pride the desirable belonging is already looked at from the point of view of what it can do for the owner, so that the self is already in his mind when he attends to it. There is here of course no implication of a temporal order, and in particular the point does not imply that in order to have a chance of being proud of this or that a person must already be in a certain frame of mind and actually be on the look-out for possible objects to give him a boost. This would only be one case among others.[16] The point is simply that a full account of pride needs a reference to the specific way of looking at the thing in question. It is partly at least because this reference is lacking that Davidson's account of pride remains unexplanatory and unconvincing. Davidson's account was in the form of a syllogism: ('Hume's Cognitive Theory of Pride' p. 751) all beautiful-house-owners are praiseworthy, I am a beautiful-house-owner, so *qua* house-owner I am praiseworthy. I have already in an earlier chapter pointed out the lack of explanatory force of the universal premiss. This point is now reinforced, for what is needed for the explanation of a particular case of pride is not reference to a universal, but needs reference rather to a particular state of mind and a particular set of expectations. Only this reference can explain why pride is an emotion rather than a set of detached judgements.

Hume, after giving his definition of pride and his list of limitations or constraints, concludes this section with the observation that it is a consequence of his account 'that the persons, who are proudest, and who in the eyes of the world have most reason for their pride, are not always the happiest; nor the most humble the most miserable' (294). He explains this point by reference to the constraints on his definition. We may, for instance, be exposed to plenty of misery the causes of which are not related to us in the way the causes of what we are proud of must be related to us. This is true enough. But Hume's conclusion, that those who frequently feel proud are not necessarily happy, follows more directly from the account of pride I have just given than it does from his five limitations. For the reference to a norm of expectations may depress as well as provide a boost, and in particular it may depress precisely by providing a boost. For it may reveal that what I view as an achievement is not so regarded by others. Tougher, brighter, more efficient people take that sort of thing in their stride. Here the mere fact of my being proud of something shows up my deficiency. In such a case I operate with two scales: my view of my own abilities and

[16] For an example of an extreme case here, see Henry James, *Washington Square*, Chapter II: 'Dr. Sloper would have liked to be proud of his daughter; but there was nothing to be proud of in poor Catherine. There was nothing, of course, to be ashamed of; but this was not enough for the Doctor, who was a proud man, and would have enjoyed being able to think of his daughter as an unusual girl.'

standing, in the light of which it is splendid to have done that thing, and the view of the matter which I believe is taken by tougher and better people, from whose point of view what I have done is not splendid at all, and the difference between the two scales may strike me as humiliating. If there are many occasions when my feeling proud is based on what I take to be my inferior norm of expectations then the seeds of unhappiness are built into my very disposition to feel proud on so many occasions. It is therefore true that we cannot infer a person being happy from the frequency of his experiencing pride. It is also true, and follows from the same considerations, that frequently feeling proud is quite compatible with taking a lowly view of oneself, and hence quite compatible with being a humble person.

4

Pride in all its forms concerns the status of the self. The different forms of pride can be explained and related to each other by reference to the view the agent takes of himself and his standing. Here it is again useful to speak of his 'norm of expectations'. A person's norm of expectations gives us his conception of his standing in society, his abilities, and so on, and so provides that which accounts for both the similarities and the dissimilarities between different kinds of pride.

The person who is proud of some possession sees owning that thing as being beyond his norm of expectations. The person who is simply proud does not view that in virtue of which he is proud (his social, financial, intellectual, moral standing) as an achievement. It is on the contrary something he takes for granted and may unthinkingly accept. He believes that the sort of person which these kinds of expectations help to identify is a superior sort of person. Very roughly, where the norm of expectations is based on his own abilities, performance, or possessions he will pitch his expectations high and take it for granted that it is at this level he operates. He thinks the norm superior in two ways: it is superior as a norm among others, i.e., the area where his expectations lie is superior compared with other possible areas; and given this, within that area his expectations are superior to possible other expectations in that specific area. If for example he expects to be a house-owner then he will expect to be the owner of a beautiful house, rather than of any old house. If the norm reflects what he believes to be generally expected in a certain area, then he may grade it high or low; if he grades it low he will think his own performance etc. to be above it as a matter of course; if he grades it high he will think his own position to be naturally at least on that level. Again, he will regard this second kind of norm as at all relevant only if it touches on his areas of interest, which as such are themselves superior areas.

It seems likely that this initial distinction between the one who is and the one who feels proud (that the notion of achievement is central to one case and does not apply to the other) will have consequences which can then be listed as further differences between the two cases. It is plausible, for instance, that comparison with others should be an essential feature of one case and not of the other. But while there is truth in this suggestion, matters are not quite so straightforward: the two cases of pride can each be subdivided and comparison with others cuts across this subdivision.

The characterization of the proud man as I gave it earlier does imply a comparison with others, for he saw his position in the hierarchy as being superior to that of others, and accepted this position as his due. But this is only one interpretation of 'seeing the superior position as due to him', and one which was natural in the context of the example of a social hierarchy. Here the person concerned sees the superior position as due to him in the sense of having high-pitched expectations of himself and others in their treatment of him the fulfilment of which he takes for granted. He expects more for and of himself than he thinks it suitable to expect of and for those whose position is inferior to his. Mr. Darcy, a typical case of this kind of pride, expects to be treated in certain ways. So he is surprised when he is informally accosted by Mr. Collins, a man greatly inferior to him in status. He expects to find himself in only certain kinds of company: he is disgusted with the society of local inhabitants at the village dance. And he also has certain expectations of himself, such as to fulfil to the best of his ability the duties of landowner and landlord. It is characteristic of this proud man that he thinks himself superior all round, i.e., he thinks that where he excels is both what is essential to and enough for being altogether superior. It is not just that he thinks his social status, or his taste, or his learning is superior to that of others; he also takes it for granted that these characteristics are so central to superiority that nothing else will count: he is superior in the areas that matter and in the only areas that matter. If there is some respect in which another excels and he does not, then this is neither here nor there as far as the superiority of his position is concerned.[17]

It is, however, possible to interpret 'superior position' as resting not on a comparison with others, but on a comparison of standards. A person may be proud in that, for instance, he will not accept help from others who are better off than he is. He does not necessarily think of himself as being superior to others at all; he merely accepts certain standards the lowering of which he would regard as a threat to his self-respect. He takes it for granted that the expectations generated by such standards will or should be fulfilled. He will, of course, behave in certain ways, and he is entitled to certain sorts of treatment from others. The person who is proud in the first sense will also be proud in this sense. But the converse is not true, for a person may have his pride without thinking himself superior to others.

There is a similar distinction to be drawn in the case of the person feeling proud. The person feeling proud need not, of course, regard his norm of expectations as in any way superior, nor need he think that he normally lives up to what is generally expected in some area of activity. In his case any comparison of his status with that of others will be incidental. Seeing his standing in a certain relationship to some object or person as an achievement implies that at the time of experiencing pride some comparison is in his mind, but this comparison is of his present elevated state with his less elevated norm, and so is primarily self-directed. This is so particularly where the norm is based on his own ability and performances: he has done better than he expected and so experiences a boost to his self-confidence. If, however, the norm of expectations refers to what he believes is generally expected in a certain area then it

---

[17] Dr. Sloper realizes this and sees here the solution to the problem he has with his daughter: he decides that paternity is, after all, not an exciting vocation, and so not an aspect of life to which he need pay much attention (Chapter XV).

seems that there must be some comparison with others, for it is against their norm of expectations that he experiences the boost. He may feel proud of his skill in handling some situation; the degree of skill, he thinks, goes beyond what is normally expected on such occasions. So he is pleased with himself. But the norm of expectations is used by him as a foil against which his fine performance can be seen to shine, and the comparison may again be wholly self-directed: he looks at his performance as compared with what it might have been and finds that it is better than anybody was entitled to expect. So he has reason to be satisfied with himself. Only this much is implied by his seeing what he has brought about as an achievement of his. But on the other hand, his realization that he is performing at a level above that generally expected may naturally lead to the thought that there is more to him than there is to others and that he therefore can think more of himself than he need think of them. In this case his feeling proud does involve a direct comparison of his status with that of others.

It seems, then, that a comparison with others may or may not occur in either case of pride. Nevertheless, there is this difference: where a person is proud in the sense in which Mr. Darcy is proud then such comparison is essential to his characterization. It is, however, never essential to the characterization of the person who feels proud, though in certain circumstances a comparison with others may as a matter of fact be involved.

Hume, as we have seen, was concerned with the moral implications of being or feeling proud. While in his view pride is not necessarily vicious, he also thinks that excessive pride is always vicious and is universally hated (592). As he does not distinguish clearly between pride the passion and pride the character-trait, it is not entirely clear what he has in mind here. Sometimes he refers to the proud man who thinks himself superior and tends to induce in us a disagreeable and mortifying feeling of inferiority (595). If this is the sort of case he is thinking of when he speaks of excessive pride as vicious then we can take him to mean that such a person's pride is excessive in that his sense of superiority goes beyond any acceptable basis for it. He may, or may not, have good grounds for thinking himself superior in this or that respect, but it does not follow that he is therefore altogether superior. The person who is proud in this sense assumes that superiority in the areas in which he excels, and in only these areas, constitutes all round superiority. But it does not follow that because he occupies a high position on some scale (social, financial, professional, etc.) he therefore is superior as a human being. If these are the sorts of considerations Hume has in mind then he is right in claiming that excessive pride is always vicious. The type of pride exemplified in Mr. Darcy is arrogance, or pride the sin.

If Hume is, however, thinking of pride the passion then it is not so clear that excessive pride is always vicious. 'Excessive' can here be interpreted in a variety of ways:

1. A person's pride may be excessive in that her thoughts dwell on herself and her achievements more often than is reasonable, by some standard. The number of times she thinks about herself is disproportionate, given all the other things there are to think about.

2. Or a person's pride may be excessive in the sense already mentioned, that she thinks well of herself on grounds which are not sufficient to support this thought. Her having done this or having acquired that is not a good reason for thinking her worth that much increased, or increased at all, or increased in that respect. The boost to her self-esteem is out of proportion to the merit of what she has or has done.

3. Finally, a person's pride may be excessive in the way in which that of the arrogant is excessive. This is where she sees herself as excelling against the background of the general norm of expectations and takes this to indicate her superiority to others. The boost, her increased self-esteem, consists in this feeling of superiority. Her pride is excessive because she takes this supposedly superior performance to increase her value as a person.

Not all forms of excessive pride are necessarily vicious. In particular, if 'excessive' has the sense of the second interpretation it is quite likely to be silly but harmless. The extent of Sir William's pride in his knighthood is no doubt unreasonable, but there is nothing vicious about it; Sir William is merely rather foolish in this respect. Neither this nor the first interpretation implies that the person concerned thinks himself superior to others. Excessive pride in its first sense is indeed quite compatible with a person thinking herself inferior. It may be precisely because she takes her expectations of her own performance to be below the general norm of expectations in some area or areas that she thinks about herself so often. Maybe this is a case of excessive pride being vicious; it at any rate suggests an undue degree of self-preoccupation.

It is excessive pride as finally interpreted which yields a vice analogous to arrogance: the person whose increased self-esteem consists in feeling superior is *par excellence* the conceited person. Sir William is not conceited because thinking himself elevated above his former position has for him merely the implication that he must change his way of life. He does not think that his position *vis-à-vis* others has changed, that he is now superior and entitled to look down on them.

Excessive pride may, then, constitute one or the other of the two vices, conceit and arrogance, depending on the kind of pride we have in mind. It is of the essence of him who is wholly arrogant that he takes his superiority for granted and so does not concern himself with any kind of evidence for his superiority. Once he starts looking for or weighing such evidence he is no longer wholly arrogant. Consequently, he need not give much thought to his excellence, and so not give much thought to himself and his status. For that is quite secure. It is far otherwise for him who is conceited. He is proud of himself, of his qualities or deeds. In Hume's terminology, the self is both cause and object of the emotion. The self is therefore doubly in his mind, and he necessarily does give thought to himself and his status. Further, the conceited person does not take his superiority for granted in the way the arrogant do. He maintains his flattering view of himself by seeing himself as thrown into relief against what he takes the ordinary norm to be, a manoeuvre which is quite unnecessary for the arrogant. In this sense the conceited are in need of evidence, in the shape of the comparative inferiority of others. Compared with the achievements of others his own are infinitely superior, he thinks, and his self-esteem can rise as his esteem for others diminishes. A pure case of conceit is therefore quite different from a pure case of arrogance—which is not to say that a person cannot be both arrogant and conceited. He may be arrogant in that he takes it totally for granted that he is superior to a certain set of people: it goes without saying that his norm operates on a higher level than does theirs. But he may also be conceited in that he thinks his performance excels by comparison with the norm of a more elevated set of people.

A person who is conceited suffers from pride which is excessive in the third sense of that phrase. But his pride is quite likely to be excessive also in the other senses. As he is proud of himself, his thoughts are quite likely to dwell on himself to a disproportionate degree; and being so concerned with his superiority he is likely also to exaggerate the grounds for such feelings, or even to fabricate them. A case in point here is Dickens's Mr. Bounderby who, in order to establish a norm against which his present position of banker and manufacturer in Coketown appears as a splendid achievement, invents a suitable background for himself. He claims to have risen from the gutter, and misses no opportunity for pointing out his remarkable rise from such unpromising beginnings:

'Tell Josiah Bounderby of Coketown, of your district schools and your model schools, and your training schools, and your whole kettle-of-fish of schools; and Josiah Bounderby of Coketown, tells you plainly, all right, all correct,—he hadn't such advantages—but let us have hard-headed, solid-fisted people—the education that made him won't do for everybody, he knows well—such and such his education was, however, and you may force him to swallow boiling fat, but you shall never force him to suppress the facts of his life.'

(*Hard Times*, Bk. I, Ch. IV.)

Mr. Bounderby is conceited, vain, and boastful. The conceited, relying as they do on the contrast with others to highlight their excellence, are for this reason also more likely to be vain, i.e., to look for the applause of others, than are the arrogant. Not needing the assurance of a favourable contrast these can afford to remain indifferent to the view of their inferiors. They need not parade their superiority, they are superior to that. They are in this respect quite self-sufficient and may indeed resent praise and applause. Shakespeare's Coriolanus, for example, finds it humiliating to be thanked and praised for his splendid deeds: of course he has fought heroically, that goes without saying for a Roman of his station. Being thanked for having done so implies that he did something more than could be expected of him as a matter of course. Those who see themselves shine against a general norm of expectations are less likely to feel insulted by praise which confirms their view of themselves, and so affords an occasion for experiencing the pleasure which is pride. Boasting is at least an attempt to bring one's excellence to the world's attention, to gain its applause and admiration, and the attempt may be crowned by success:

It was one of the most exasperating attributes of Bounderby, that he not only sang his own praises but stimulated other men to sing them. There was a moral infection of clap-trap in him. Strangers, modest enough elsewhere, started up at dinners in Coketown, and boasted, in quite a rampant way, of Bounderby. (Bk. I, Ch. VII.)

It is then not surprising to find the conceited both vain and boastful. But it is nevertheless possible to be conceited and not vain, just as it is possible to be vain and arrogant. He who takes his superior position for granted need not thereby be prevented from welcoming public acknowledgement of this state.[18]

Excessive pride may then indeed be vicious, but Hume is not right in saying that it is always so. While arrogance is implied in the characterization of one form of pride, conceit is only contingently related to pride the passion. There is still one form of pride mentioned earlier which it is hard to see as being excessive in any way at all. In that sense a person was proud in that she had her pride, she was too proud to do this or accept that. This sort of pride has by itself nothing to do with feeling superior or with experiencing self-satisfaction; far from having even a hint of viciousness about it, it would seem to be a virtue. Earlier I characterized such pride in terms of standards which, in the agent's view, it was necessary for her to adhere to if she was to keep her self-respect. If it is true that self-respect is one of the most important human goods[19] then it may be that it is the lack of such pride rather than any form of it which is vicious.

There is a link between this kind of pride and feeling shame, and a link also between it and a person's integrity. So I shall return to it in later chapters. Whether such pride is in fact a virtue will no doubt depend on the sorts of standards which are

---

[18] Hume's point, that what a person is proud of should be discernible to others as well as himself, is true of those who are vain.

[19] Rawls speaks of self-respect as probably the most important primary good, *A Theory of Justice* (OUP, 1973), p. 440.

involved in the particular case. For it includes 'false' as well as 'true' or 'proper' pride. What is false and what is proper can of course be variously assessed. It may be that one sort of false pride is a feature of the arrogant who are too proud to act in certain ways or to accept some treatment from others because they hold these others in such contempt. But this is only one possible case. In general, pride is regarded as false if it involves a muddled value-judgement, a setting too much store by some things and not enough by others.[20] By contrast, proper pride is thought to be based on sound values. The person who has this kind of pride will value himself as he ought, i.e., what he is too proud to do or accept is what ought not to be done or accepted. If this is what we are to understand by 'proper pride' then the possession of it is a virtue. It is then a kind of pride which is not to be contrasted with humility but which on the contrary coincides with humility the (Christian) virtue. The humble who occupy and accept a lowly position on some hierarchical scale may be merely poor and meek. But to be virtuously humble is not to accept meekly just any sort of inferior position. Aquinas thinks of humility as that virtue which tempers and restrains the mind 'lest it tends to high things immoderately'. Not to be immoderate in one's striving does not imply that one must be satisfied with anything that is lowly, it may on the contrary be quite wrong to do so, 'for instance', Aquinas continues, 'when man "not understanding his honour, compares himself to senseless beasts, and becomes like to them" (Ps. xlviii. 13)' (*Summa Theologica*, II. ii. Q. 161, Art. 1). Being virtuously humble does not mean losing one's human dignity and self-respect. The humble will still 'have their pride', still think that a certain kind of treatment is due to them, and that a certain kind of behaviour on their part is due to others. They will get right what kind of treatment to give and to expect.

In structure humility the virtue is not strictly the polar opposite to sinful pride, whether this is taken to be arrogance or

[20] Coriolanus who does not want to show his wounds to the Roman citizens he despises illustrates the first case of false pride. A rather different sort of false pride comes from Trollope's *Framley Parsonage*. Mr. Crawley: 'It would not hurt you to see me at your table with worn shoes and a ragged shirt. I do not think so meanly of you as that . . . But it would hurt me to know that there were those looking at me who thought me unfit to sit in your rooms.' Mr. Arabin: 'That is the pride of which I speak; false pride.' (Ch. XXXVI.)

conceit. The person possessing humility need neither take it for granted that he is inferior to others nor discover himself to be so by comparison with them; he may not think in terms of comparison with others at all. That is to say, some kinds of comparison, for instance, that he occupies a socially inferior position, will not for him have much significance, for he will not assume that such things are constitutive of human worth. Comparisons which are significant in that in his view they indicate his own moral inferiority are not essential to the characterization of the humble as reference to comparative superiority is to that of the proud. Where pride and humility are of course opposites is in the view the proud and the humble respectively take of themselves and therefore of others. The humble, unlike the proud, will not exalt himself above others, nor will he be complacent about himself. He will therefore not suffer from that blindness towards both the worth of others and his own defects which is so characteristic of sinful pride.

III

SHAME

IT seems prima facie plausible that shame (and not as Hume claims, 'humility') is the polar opposite of emotional pride, and so it would seem that this emotion raises no structural difficulties other than those already encountered. At least, 'feeling ashamed of something' corresponds in grammatical form to 'feeling proud of something', and the explanatory beliefs accounting for my feeling ashamed will be analogous to those which explained my feeling proud: what I am ashamed of I regard as in some respect undesirable and as connected to me in one of the possible ways discussed. But if it is the phenomenon of shame that is to be isolated then a comparison between feeling ashamed and feeling proud is not altogether to the point. To speak of someone as feeling ashamed is not to be very specific about his state. In particular, feeling ashamed may or may not be feeling shame. It is quite possible for a person to claim sincerely that he is feeling ashamed of having said or done something where this means no more than that he regrets having done that thing. 'I am ashamed of it' may function as an expression of regret or remorse which does not involve any beliefs on the agent's part concerning his own standing. Feeling shame, on the other hand, does seem to involve such a belief and so to be in this respect analogous to pride. But although there is thus some justification in linking pride and shame, the latter nevertheless has features which give rise to new problems. It introduces first of all the notion of an audience, for feeling shame is connected with the thought that eyes are upon one. And further, there is a suggestion made by a number of philosophers that there are different kinds of shame, that we should distinguish between forward-looking and backward-looking shame, or between spiritual and physical shame, or

again between moral and natural shame.[1] What these philosophers primarily have in mind is that in one case, but not in the
other, there is an appeal to some moral standard in the light of
which the agent is judged or judges himself adversely. Sometimes, according to them, we feel shame on the grounds that we
have done or thought something we regard as bad. But at other
times we feel shame not for this reason at all, but feel it rather
because we think of ourselves as being seen on an occasion
when being seen is an intrusion of one's privacy and so objec-
tionable. But here there is not, or need not be, any question of
moral censure. Such a distinction between kinds of shame
would suggest that shame, or at least one kind, is related to
moral standards in a way in which pride is not, so that it but
not pride may properly be labelled a 'moral emotion'.

I do not, of course, wish to deny that there are very different
cases of shame. But I think it mistaken to speak here of different
kinds, if this implies that these differ from each other in crucial
features. The difference between these cases is in fact quite
superficial; basically they all share the same structure.

1

As in the case of pride and humility it is again useful to introduce a framework within which the characterization of shame
can be pinned down crudely but with relatively clarity. In this
case such a framework is provided by what anthropologists call
a 'shame-culture'. The distinguishing mark of such a culture,
and that which makes it different from a so-called 'guilt-culture',
is that here public esteem is the greatest good, and to be ill
spoken of the greatest evil. Public esteem for the individual, or
the lack of it, depends on that individual's success or failure
judged on the basis of some code which embodies that society's
values. Whoever fails to meet the categoric demands engendered
by that code ruins his reputation and loses the esteem of the
other members of that group. He loses his honour. The notion
of honour here is clearly that of public reputation. We think it

[1] These suggestions come respectively from: Otto Friedrich Bollnow, *Die Ehrfurcht*
(Klostermann, Frankfurt, 1958), Chs. III and IV; Max Scheler, *Schriften aus dem
Nachlass; Zur Ethik und Bekenntnislehre* (Francke Verlag, Bern, 1957), Band I, 'Über
Scham und Schamgefühle'; and John Rawls, *A Theory of Justice*, Part 3, Ch. VII.

quite possible to ask whether a man whose reputation is immense does in fact possess those qualities because of which we should regard him as a man of honour; we may suspect that he is corrupt. We distinguish between the 'externals' of honour, the reputation and distinction accorded to him on the basis of virtues he is assumed to have, and the actual possession of such virtuous qualities. A man may have either one without the other. But such distinctions do not make sense in a shame-culture. One is tempted to say that what is of overriding importance here for every member of the group is how he appears in public, never mind the inner man; but this formulation implies precisely that distinction between appearance and reality, between public and private, which is unacceptable within the framework of the shame-culture. If public esteem is the sole value, to which whatever else may be valued is related as means to end, then it follows that where there is no public esteem there is no value. Hence if a man has lost his reputation then he has lost his value in the eyes of all the members of the group, and this includes himself. So there is nothing left, no inner quality or whatever, which could be judged to be of value in spite of the loss of public respect. Self-respect and public respect stand and fall together. There can be no distinction between private and public; for on the present hypothesis a person can assess himself only in terms of what the public thinks of him. The 'public' in this case constitutes an honour-group. Membership of the group is determined by the relation in which individuals stand to each other. If this relationship is governed by the relevant honour-code then we have members of the same group; if not, then not. An example often quoted are the heroes in Homer's *Iliad*.[2] They form an honour-group: they expect certain types of behaviour of themselves and others, and judge themselves and others accordingly. Traders and slaves do not of course belong to that honour-group. Nor for that matter do the gods. Although they, like the heroes, set great store by public esteem, they are not crushed when this is not forthcoming but are rather resentful and angry. They do not see themselves as having been condemned, but merely as having been slighted. Membership of the group, then, is judged

[2] See E. R. Dodds, *The Greek and the Irrational* (University of California Press, 1951), Ch. II.

on the basis of a value-system to which any individual owes its status as a member. But membership allows him no status at all as an individual which is in any way independent of his member-status. Hence, if he loses his status as a member he also loses his status as an individual. Loss of honour is total extinction of the individual that existed as a member of the group, it is total loss of identity. Not surprisingly, loss of honour in a shame-culture is the worst that can happen to any woman or man.

So to be dishonoured it is necessary to belong to an honour-group in the first place: it may happen to the hero, but cannot happen to the slave. He will be dishonoured if he is judged to have failed to meet whatever is demanded by the code. What the failure consists in depends on what the values of the society are. Dishonour may attach to poverty or to the feebleness of old age, i.e., to something which may befall anyone through no fault of his own. Or it may attach to what is brought about by the person's own behaviour, such as cowardice in men and lack of chastity in women. But whatever it may be, the code will be sufficiently well articulated for members to recognize failure to comply. Where there is no such code, terms like 'honour' and 'shame' will lack a clear application.

An individual is dishonoured when he is judged by the group of which he is a member to have failed to comply with some categoric demand. He himself shares the point of view of the group, and so he has failed in his own eyes. This is so necessarily: being a member of the group entails being held in esteem by the group, and being held in esteem entails both that certain demands are made on him and that he has certain claims. These demands and claims, i.e., these mutual expectations, are generated by the value-system by reference to which the group is identified as one group. So these expectations, and they alone, are what confers value on the individual. As a member of the group every individual must see himself and others in this light, otherwise he would not be a member of this group. It follows that for any individual a breakdown of his various expectations must involve his total loss of value in his own eyes.

The shame-culture with its honour-code and consequent demands on the individual provides a clear case of what it is for one of its members to be shamed: he is seen to have failed to meet the demands. The feeling of shame is the response on the part of the agent to the situation seen in this way. He accepts the resultant judgement; he is dishonoured in his own eyes. Of course, feelings of shame nowadays and in our culture are unlikely to occur under such specific circumstances. Nevertheless, the essential features are preserved in the structure of shame. That it is the view of the public and public esteem which is all-important is reflected in the thought that shame requires an audience. The agent is seen as deviating from some norm, and in feeling shame he will identify with the audience's view and the consequent verdict that he has lost status.

2

The person who feels proud needs to be self-conscious in the sense that he must have some awareness of his position in the world, and have some conception of his worth, however inarticulate that might be. The self-consciousness required for shame, however, seems to be of a higher order than this. The person feeling shame feels exposed: he thinks of himself as being seen through the eyes of another. The case of shame introduces an observer or audience, as the case of pride did not. Sartre, in *Being and Nothingness*, gives us an example of shame which underlines this point: a man makes a vulgar gesture.[3] He then realizes that he is being observed. This realization makes him look at what he is doing through the observer's eyes. Seeing it from that point of view he realizes that what he is doing is vulgar, and he feels shame. Here we have an observer who, the agent realizes, watches him and judges his action adversely. The agent accepts the judgement and thereby accepts the standard or values involved. So he realizes that he is capable of a vulgar action, and this degrades him in his own eyes. The structure of this case can be compared to that of a member of an honour-group in a shame-culture losing his status, or losing honour. In both cases we have the identification of agent with audience: they both see the situation alike and judge it to be a deviation from the accepted norm. Con-

[3] Part 3, Ch. I (translation H. E. Barnes, Methuen, 1969).

sequently, in the eyes of both the agent is degraded. In Sartre's case the agent and his observer form, for the moment at least, a mini honour-group. The crucial point is that only by seeing what he is doing through the other's eyes does he recognize the nature of his action, and so it is crucial, it seems, that there be some other through whose eyes he can look at his action.

Sartre introduces an actual observer watching the behaviour of the agent. But it is plainly untrue that all cases of feeling shame are cases of public exposure, untrue, that is, that an actual observer is required for shame to be felt. Nor is it true even that the agent must believe, rightly or wrongly, that he is being observed by some other person. One may feel shame when quite alone and knowing this to be so. It has recently been argued that the weaker claim, that shame involves imagining an audience, is not correct, either: 'it is quite possible to think of people, such as writers and craftsmen, with high standards of their own, feeling shame just because they have let themselves down (not produced a masterpiece), without thinking of them imagining other craftsmen inspecting and condemning their work.'[4]

It is certainly true that to feel shame about his inferior work a craftsman need not think, i.e., either believe or imagine, *that there is* another craftsman looking at his work. He need not imagine an actual observer, and that there is such an observer need not be part of the content of his thought. All that seems necessary is that he shift his viewpoint from that of the creator of the work to that of the critical assessor, and he himself can fulfil both these functions.

Yet the point that there is a shifting point of view involved in the occurrence of shame is not enough to account for the thought that shame requires an audience, that shame is somehow connected with exposure. The shift is not only in the view the craftsman takes of his work, it is also in the view he takes of himself. This is so at least if he really feels shame. It may be that this craftsman merely feels ashamed of his work. In that case the notion of an audience need not be appealed to at all, for feeling ashamed of his work requires merely that he recognize that not all is well with it and that he ought to do better.

---

[4] Anthony O'Hear, 'Guilt and Shame as Moral Concepts', *Proceedings Aristotelean Society* 1976–7, p. 77.

His thoughts will be primarily on his work. But a person feeling shame becomes conscious not merely of what he is doing, but becomes conscious also of his self. This means partly that he cannot be unselfconscious in the manner of a young child or of somebody wholly absorbed in what he is doing. But it is also the self-consciousness of Adam and Eve after the fall: 'the eyes of both were opened, and they knew that they were naked.' (Genesis 3: 7). If neither the believed nor the imagined presence of another is required then it appears that it may be the agent's own eyes to which he feels himself exposed. It may indeed be that it *must* be the agent's own eyes which constitute the audience, for he is supposed to identify with the audience. The Sartre example makes this point: the man's identification with the observer is taken to mean that he now also sees his action as making a vulgar gesture, and condemns it under this description and himself as capable of such an action. The agent looks at his own action through the observer's eyes and so it is suddenly revealed to him what it amounts to. The observer is merely the means towards this end, and as such he is dispensable. It is a mistake to think of the actual observer as being the audience.

It seems that we now have a dilemma: 'shame requires an audience' is given either too much or too little content; it is given too much if we insist on at least the imagined presence of another. But if all it requires is that one should occupy an observer's position *vis-à-vis* oneself then the metaphors of eyes being upon one or being revealed to an audience seem to be rather heavy machinery for making just this point. The problem therefore is to give adequate content to the notion of the audience without introducing what is conceptually irrelevant to feeling shame.

Sartre's example suggests that we need two *dramatis personae*: the actor and the audience or observer who both sees and criticizes. The actor then identifies with the audience in that he also sees and criticizes. This is an over-simplification of the state of affairs. It is this view which leads either to an account of shame which is misleading because at best it covers only a limited range of cases, or it tempts philosophers to distinguish between different kinds of shame, where only one kind requires a critical audience. The mistake here is to over-simplify the notion of the audience. If we take Sartre's example as a paradigm case of shame then the over-simplification is twofold: firstly, the example implies that the observer is critical of the agent. But this is only one possibility; the audience required for shame need not be thought of as critical at all. And secondly, the agent accepts what he takes to be the observer's description of what he is doing. But this, too, is only one possibility; a person may feel shame and yet reject the audience's description of his position, and thereby also reject the adverse judgement of what he is doing if the audience is a critical one. An account of shame which remedies these faults and appeals to a more complex notion of the audience will be both uniform in that it will cover all cases of shame, and will also explain how much content is to be given to the thought that shame requires an audience.

The point about the audience is that it occupies an observer and not a participant position. Unlike the agent, the audience is detached. It is reference to just this basic notion of the audience which is primarily needed for an explanation of shame: in feeling shame the actor thinks of himself as having become an object of detached observation, and at the core to feel shame is to feel distress at being seen at all. *How* he is seen, whether he thinks of the audience as critical, approving, indifferent, cynical or naïve is a distinguishable step and accounts for the different cases of shame.

That the thought of being seen at all may be enough for feeling shame is too familiar a suggestion to need much support. In some circumstances it seems wrong to the agent to be an object of observation at all to any or to some particular sort of audience. The convent girl thinks she ought not to be seen by the young man, but the grounds for this thought are not, or need not be, that she believes he would be critical of her. What does need support is that in a case like that of the convent girl there is what might be labelled a judging audience as well as a seeing one, and that in cases of condemnation as in the Sartre example different kinds of audiences should be distinguished.

As on my account both these cases have precisely the same structure a defence of either position will turn out to be a defence of the other as well. For illustration I shall adapt an example suggested by Scheler (*Shriften ans dem Nachlass*, p. 79).

A model who has been posing for an artist for some time comes to feel shame when she realizes that he no longer regards her as a model, but regards her as a woman. We have here to begin with a position in which she is at ease: she thinks, or unthinkingly assumes, that their relation is a wholly impersonal one. She then becomes aware of a changed point of view on the part of the artist, which is a view that clashes with the one held by her, or unthinkingly assumed by her. Awareness of this view forces her to abandon her own view of the situation, viz., forces her to see their relation as no longer impersonal. She does not, however, need to see herself as the artist sees her, she need not see herself as a woman in the sense of 'object of sexual interest'. She merely becomes aware that she is so seen. So in this respect she does not identify with the audience, she sees rather how she appears to the artist. Nor need she think of that audience's viewpoint as being at all critical of her; it is more likely in the circumstances that his attitude is one of approval. However, she must identify with some critical view of herself if we are to have a case of shame. For this feeling remains unexplained by merely the reference to the fact that she now thinks of herself as being seen differently. To this, if she reacts emotionally at all, she may react with all sorts of other emotions. She may feel anger or resentment, or she may feel pleased or proud.

The model need not see herself as the artist sees her. But as the result of realizing her relation to him she sees herself in a new light. The point can be expressed by introducing a second, higher order point of view from which she is seen not as an object of sexual interest, but is seen as *being seen* as such an object. With this point of view she does identify, and this point of view is a critical one. The adverse judgement, however, comes not from the artist, but comes from herself. It is critical in that it pronounces it wrong for her to be so seen, at least at this time and by this audience. Being seen as she is seen is to be in a position in which no decent woman should find herself. As the case is given this is no fault of hers, but the question of responsibility is irrelevant to feelings of shame. However it may have come about, she is now in a false position and for this she is condemned.

A closely analogous account can be applied to cases where shame may be thought to prevent a person from acting in a certain way. So for instance it will offer an at least plausible account of Cordelia's behaviour in the Abdication scene: Cordelia is required to tell her father how much she loves him. For reasons of his own Lear wants her publicly to demonstrate her love for him. She refuses to do so. Her task is, in her view, an impossible one: the fine speeches just made by her sisters seem to be the thing required, but they most certainly are not demonstrations of love. The love Cordelia feels for her father can perhaps not be put into words at all, and in any case cannot be demonstrated by such speeches. We have here an actual audience: Lear and his court and family. Very likely Cordelia thinks of this audience as being cynical rather than naïve; she takes it that they know perfectly well what such fine speeches are worth: they will secure each daughter a part of the kingdom. An audience of this kind will cynically expect Cordelia to act as her sisters did. So, Cordelia realizes, were she to respond in the apparently required way she would be thought by this audience to be no better than her sisters. But she knows herself to be better than her sisters are, so she would not accept this description as true of herself, she would not identify with this audience. Yet from a higher order point of view she sees that by making a fine speech in public her relation to that audience would change. If she acts as she is cynically expected to do she would make common cause with that audience and no longer be able to dissociate herself from it. But the audience is a worthless lot, taking it for granted that self-interest and gain are the only reasons for action. So from this point of view Cordelia sees herself as being seen as one of that worthless lot, and with that point of view she does identify. In aligning herself with them she would lower herself to their level. She would then find herself in a shameful position, and shame prevents her from acting as she is cynically expected to do. Her silence protects herself and her position *vis-à-vis* the audience.[5]

I have made the actual audience here a cynical one, but the case is only slightly altered if Cordelia thinks of it as naïve or quite indifferent. To try and articulate her love for her father in

---

[5] Cordelia may be feeling shame at the thought that she might be making common cause with her sisters, or she may think she would feel shame if she did. Either alternative seems possible. Perhaps they cannot be clearly distinguished.

front of an indifferent audience may seem to her enough to spoil it and to leave her in the position of the spoiler of her love. The attitude ascribed to an actual or imagined audience will alter a case of shame only superficially and not structurally. The important point is that she realizes that were she to act as required she would be seen by the audience under a certain description; what this description is will depend on what attitude she believes the audience to have. This is exactly analogous to the case of the model; Cordelia merely introduces the extra complication that she does not find herself in but merely envisages herself in the shameful situation.[6]

The cases of Cordelia and the model are more complex than is that of the man in Sartre's example. He identifies with the audience in the sense of accepting the observer's description as true of what he is doing. But even so it is not necessary to think of the audience as critical: the observer may not in the least condemn the agent's vulgarity, he may on the contrary now find himself much more at ease in the man's company. And it may be precisely the awareness of this change of attitude on the part of the observer which makes the agent realize how degraded his position now is. Earlier I spoke of actor and audience as forming a mini honour-group. This now turns out to have more than one interpretation: it may be that the agent believes the audience to judge him by some standard which they share, and so he accepts the critical judgement. Or it may be that

[6] At least *this* shameful situation she only envisages. She may well also find herself in a shameful situation of a different kind: Lear seems to be inviting deception and so to be debasing what is valuable, and does not even seem to be aware that this is what he is doing. This is a doubly shameful position for Lear to be in, and as his daughter Cordelia must be implicated. And this is how she sees the situation: to be the daughter of a shameless father is to find oneself in a shameful position. As a daughter she should honour and respect him, but he takes the ground from under her feet. So he ruins the proper father-daughter relationship. But a 'proper' father and a 'proper' daughter are defined in terms of such a relationship. Thus Cordelia can hardly be a proper daughter to such a father, and so her own status has been undermined. Here the behaviour of another is the catalyst for her shame. As in the case of pride, this is possible only because Cordelia sees herself as 'connected' to Lear, viz., by family ties. Being so connected is sufficient for her own degradation, although of course she has done nothing to deserve this. There are many possible variations of the Cordelia case in a setting where family honour plays an important role. So one might explain Desdemona's passivity in the face of Othello's accusation by her conception of what constitutes a 'proper' wife. The belief on Othello's part, that she has committed adultery, is enough to undermine this position and enough, therefore, for loss of honour. That the belief is in fact unfounded is not of crucial relevance.

being seen in a certain way forces him to join the audience's 'honour-group', and it is this which he judges degrading. It may also be the case that the agent sees himself judged by standards he thinks he ought to share, and he feels shame because he is not, for example, a good enough person to share them.

If we take the description of the features of shame as we find them in Sartre's example as the description of the paradigm case, then it turns out that we cannot accommodate more complex but still quite ordinary cases of shame without adding all sorts of qualifications. This is not therefore a particularly attractive approach; it is not only untidy but also misleading about what is involved in feeling shame. The alternative is to start the other way round and treat Sartre's example as a specific case of shame falling under a more complex general description.

There are basically two elements in each case of shame. There is firstly the self-directed adverse judgement of the person feeling shame: she feels herself degraded, not the sort of person she believed, assumed, or hoped she was or anyway should be. This judgement is constitutive of the emotion, it is the person's identificatory belief. Secondly, there is the notion of the audience. This notion has a role to play in the explanation of the self-directed judgement. The notion of the audience is, as we have seen, itself complex. It consists of two distinguishable points of view. The first point of view audience sees the agent under some description, which may or may not entail some assessment of the agent. The seeing may be indifferent or friendly or hostile in some way. The attitude of the audience is therefore not to be identified with the agent's own attitude to herself, which in a case of shame can only be unfavourable. Even where the seeing is hostile the two should not be confused. For being seen with hostility may be perfectly acceptable to the agent if the relevant audience is one whose views she rather despises. But of course the different modes of seeing will account in different ways for the person's feeling shame. So if she feels shame although she thinks she is seen with approval then this can only be because she believes that being so seen puts her on a level with the audience, and it is this which is degrading. If on the other hand she thinks of the audience as indifferent then she will believe either that this audience does not think her worthy of attention, and this is demeaning, or she believes that on this occasion she ought not to be seen at all, or at any rate be seen only by the sympathetic. And if she thinks of the audience's seeing as hostile then this will imply that she takes very seriously (at least at the time) the standards in the light of which she is so seen. There is therefore a con- nection between the manner in which the agent is seen and the nature of her self-critical judgement.

These examples already indicate the function of the second point of view audience. This concerns itself with the relation between the agent and the first audience. It views the different forms of seeing, and always views them critically: to be so seen is to be exposed, for the agent should not be seen in this way. This point of view is always needed as a step towards the self- realization which is expressed in the person's self-directed judgement. This is plainly so in the cases of the model and of Cordelia. But it is needed also for the man making the vulgar gesture, and for the craftsman, if that craftsman is to experi- ence shame. Sartre's man is initially in a state where he is un- selfconscious. He then realizes that what he is doing can be seen under some description. Even if this description constitutes a hostile assessment of what he is doing, as we here assume it to do, this need not bring about shame rather than any other emo- tional reaction. For he may think that only the unperceptive or the despicable would see it in this way, and he is not affected by their views. He does not accept the description as being at all true of what he is really doing. The thought of it being so des- cribed may leave him indifferent or cause him to feel resentful rather than feel shame. But it is given that he does feel shame, and so he sees his being so seen as constituting adverse criti- cism of himself, which he has to accept. He has to accept it in this case because he thinks he is as he is seen, i.e., his judge- ment coincides with the judgement embodied in the observer- description. This is one possibility. The other is that although the judgements do not coincide there is nevertheless something wrong in his being so seen.

The question arose earlier what content to give to the thought that shame requires an audience. This created problems as any possible content seemed either too substantial to be required for shame, or so slight that talk of the audience seemed super- fluous. The conclusion now reached is that it is of course not necessary for feeling shame that the agent believe or imagine there to be some observer who views him under some description. The actual or imagined observer may merely be the means of making the agent look at himself, he is in no way essential. What is essential is the shift in the agent's viewpoint *vis-à-vis* himself. But this by itself is not enough, for it does not account sufficiently for the complex notion of the audience.

To speak of an audience is of course to speak metaphorically. What has been described as seen from different audience points of view is the content of some of the agent's explanatory beliefs. So on the occasion of an occurrence of shame the person believes that she is defective and degraded. This is her identificatory belief. She sees herself in these terms because she is presented with a contrast, where the contrast is between her unselfconscious state, what she thought or hoped or unthinkingly assumed she was, or was doing, and what she has now under the observer-description turned out to be. This comes as a revelation to her. But it need be a revelation only given her initial unselfconsciousness. She may not be making a new discovery about herself, it may just be a reminder. She reaches this judgement by means of her beliefs that what she is doing may be seen under some description (where the description may just be 'object of observation') and that she ought not to be so seen, it is a false position in which she finds herself. What precisely makes it a false position will of course vary according to the circumstances.

There is, then, this point to the metaphors of an audience and of being seen: they reflect the structural features of the agent's becoming aware of the discrepancy between her own assumption about her state or action and a possible detached observer-description of this state or action, and of her further being aware that she ought not to be in a position where she could be so seen, where such a description at least appears to fit. For particular cases of shame an actual or imagined observer may or may not be required. He may be required if the person feels shame because seen at all, and in other cases an actual or imagined observer may be the means of bringing about the agent's realizations. But whether or not there is, or is imagined to be, such an observer is a contingent matter. Beliefs concerning possible detached descriptions of one's action or state were not a feature of emotional pride; they introduce a dimension which that emotion lacked. But beliefs which are analogous to those enumerated in the case of pride must be present also in the case of shame if we are to understand why awareness of an observer-description has the effect it does on the agent. What the description picks out will strike her as in some respect undesirable and will refer to what is in one or another of the ways discussed closely connected with her.

Shame requires a sophisticated type of self-consciousness. A person feeling shame will exercise her capacity for self-awareness, and she will do so dramatically: from being just an actor absorbed in what she is doing she will suddenly become self-aware and self-critical. It is plainly a state of self-consciousness which centrally relies on the concept of another, for the thought of being seen as one might be seen by another is the catalyst for the emotion. The element of drama in the shifting viewpoints and the sudden realization of one's changed position is quite missing in the case of pride. The point of view, the seeing eye, is not built into the structure of pride as it is built into the structure of shame. In this, as in its general structure, humiliation is like shame and unlike pride. When feeling humiliated the agent again assesses herself in relation to how she appears to some audience or observer's point of view. The difference between the two emotions is one of emphasis: we again have the observer's point of view from which the agent is seen under a certain description. Being seen by that audience in that way implies, in the agent's view, that she is not being given the position which is due to her, or she had assumed was due to her. She therefore sees herself involved in a fall from a higher to a lower position. It is the fall itself which is here the prime concern, rather than her new degraded status. It does not matter whether the fall is a revelation of faults or weaknesses to the public eye only, or whether it is a revelation also to the agent herself. Nor does it matter whether she accepts the fall as deserved or not, whether or not she accepts that she is, for example, as corrupt or weak as she is now thought to be. She will in any case think of herself as being thought presumptuous in having allotted to herself such a high position, whether or not she shares this view. And she will think of herself as appearing contemptible or ludicrous just because she is not, in the audience's view, the sort of person she gave herself out to be. The judgement involved here is comparative, as it was in shame: it embraces both the earlier high and the new low position. But what precisely is judged adversely is different. It is that she aspired to the high position when she had no business to do so, or appeared to others to do so, and it is this thought, that she is regarded as presumptuous, which is essential to humiliation as it is not to shame.

3

A person feeling shame judges herself adversely. This judgement is brought about by the realization of how her position is or may be seen from an observer's point of view. But there is no reference to such a point of view in her final self-directed judgement. It is because the agent thinks of herself in a certain relation to the audience that she now thinks herself degraded, but she does not think of this degradation as depending on an audience. Her final judgement concerns herself only: she is degraded not relatively to this audience, she is degraded absolutely. Thinking of herself as being seen in a certain way has revealed her to herself as inferior to what she believed, assumed, or hoped to be. As what is ultimately revealed is her lower standing she naturally feels helpless and hopeless. If in her own view she is what she has just been revealed to be then there seems to be nothing she can do about it. This at least is her feeling at the moment; it does not of course necessarily persist. She may realize that she does not after all accept the standards by reference to which she has judged herself, so that she was misguided to let them be imposed on her at the time. Or she may come to change her standards, either because she comes to see that after all they are not the right ones by which to judge a person, or because she comes to think that it is absurd to judge oneself by standards which are too high to live up to. Either way of ridding oneself of shame evidently takes time, and while it may reduce the number of occasions for feeling shame in the future, it cannot alleviate the feeling of helplessness at the moment of feeling shame.

The nature of the agent's self-directed judgement, the nature of the identificatory belief, can be elucidated by contrasting it with that in the similar emotion of embarrassment. Shame and embarrassment are not usually distinguished from one another in the relevant literature.[7] This is not surprising as their structures seem very similar. Embarrassment, too, is an emotion of self-assessment and requires the necessary degree of self-consciousness. As in shame, someone absorbed in what he is doing cannot feel embarrassed. Here, too, the agent seems to be exposed to an audience, and he judges himself adversely. Yet shame strikes one as the weightier and more shattering emotion. It is connected with the agent's personal morality in a way in which embarrassment is not. Embarrassment, but not shame, implies some kind of a social context, which perhaps accounts for the fact that it may be 'catching' as shame is not. On the other hand, the element of revelation is not crucial to embarrassment and consequently visual metaphors are not so appropriate.

If so, then the role of the audience, i.e., what the explanatory beliefs are about, will be rather different in the case of embarrassment. It is true that the consciousness of being seen may be enough to cause either emotion; but the being seen is differently conceived: while in shame the agent thinks of it as a revealing of himself, in embarrassment he regards it as a demand for some response. The tension and confusion so typical of embarrassment are due to his seeing the situation as creating a demand to which he is unable to respond. Of course, there are situations of this kind where I nevertheless cannot be embarrassed. A pipe may burst and demand immediate action. Faced with this emergency I may dither as to what to do first and so fail to do what is required, and of course be fully aware of my failure. But whatever my emotional reactions under the circumstances, embarrassment can be one of them only if I believe myself to be watched, if I think or perhaps imagine that I am

[7] They are not distinguished by, e.g., Scheler, *Schriften aus dem Nachlass*; nor by E. Goffman, 'Embarrassment and Social Organisation' in *Interaction and Ritual* (Penguin University Books, 1972). Some of the examples and comments in Christopher Ricks' *Keats and Embarrassment* (OUP, 1976) are also more naturally interpreted as referring to shame rather than embarrassment. In *Die Ehrfurcht*, Bollnow disentangles a number of shame-related phenomena, but does not quite catch the area of embarrassment. The German word *verlegen*, which is the normal translation of 'embarrassed' at least over a range of cases, does not mean quite the same. Maybe, as Professor Ricks suggests, embarrassment is a typically English emotion, or at least one which the English particularly saw reason to single out and name.

seen making a mess of things. This seems to suggest that, unlike shame, embarrassment requires an embodied audience, or at least requires that the agent should imagine that such an audience is present. The demand relevant to embarrassment seems to be created not so much by the burst pipe as by the eyes which are upon me.

In the very basic and simple case where being seen is sufficient for feeling embarrassed it is indeed the being seen as such which creates the demand for a response. The person concerned, the adolescent for instance, can no longer behave 'naturally' as he did until aware of being seen. Just to be the object of observation and attention puts a stop to it and creates a new situation in which something different is required. If not just being seen, then being seen under certain circumstances or being seen from a certain point of view may create the demand for an appropriate response. To be seen by someone efficient who can deal with bursting pipes may strike me as making a demand on me, whereas being seen by someone equally helpless in such a situation may not. From that point of view possible variations in the manner of being seen are parallel to those in the audience in shame.

It seems, then, that it is the role of this audience in embarrassment to impose a demand on the agent. Often, normally perhaps, this role is played by an actual audience. But that this be so seems not necessary for embarrassment. The following case illustrates this point. Some people are gathered together for a light-hearted social evening. Suddenly one of them begins to pray; the other guests are embarrassed.[8] To be in that state, if my account so far is right, the guest must see this new situation as demanding some response of him. The claim is supported by the consideration that a guest would not on such an occasion feel embarrassed if he thought of himself as just an uninvolved spectator. He may remain quite detached, or he may feel amused, or angry that a pleasant evening has been spoilt. He may hold the praying guest or his host responsible

[8] This example is derived from one Kant is said to have used in one of his lectures, though his point was an entirely different one. In the course of explaining why a righteous man is liable to feel shame when surprised at his devotions, he remarks: 'let us assume that some one present were suddenly to uplift his hands and pray . . . we should be taken aback . . .'. 'Devoutness and the Feeling of Shame' in *Lectures on Ethics*, trans. L. Infield (Methuen, 1930).

for this state of affairs, but anyway it is not, in his view, his business to put matters right. Nor would that guest feel embarrassed who knew exactly what to do: he joins in the prayer or organizes charades. He is sure of himself and copes; he meets the demands of the situation as he sees them. The guest who is embarrassed neither remains uninvolved nor knows what to do. He thinks he ought to do something, but cannot think what, or dithers between possible alternatives. Or he may know what he ought to do (join in the prayer, for instance) but does not act accordingly, prevented perhaps by the thought that in doing so he would attract attention and thus create another embarrassing situation for himself.

For the guest to think of himself as relevantly involved does not, however, mean that he must think of himself as being seen by those present. In the case described there is of course an actual audience, and it may be that the person concerned thinks of himself as being seen by it. This would quite straightforwardly be the case if it is the host who feels embarrassed because he is aware that his guests expect him to do something to relieve the situation and he cannot think what. He fails to meet the demand imposed by the actual audience. But this is not the only possible case. The embarrassed person may be a guest who knows quite well that the others present have no particular expectations of him, that they are not paying attention to him at all. So the demand for some response does not seem to be created by those actually around him. Nevertheless, he thinks something is expected of him.

There are a number of reasons why this particular guest may feel embarrassed: he may, possibly, think himself into the position of the praying guest. He could not bear to be in his position, the object of attention and amazement. He would not be able to concentrate on his prayer, he would be distracted by his desire to be invisible to that audience. When praying he does not want to be seen at all, or at least not in the given circumstances, and were he so seen he would be in a state of confusion, not knowing whether to carry on with his prayer or somehow get himself out of that situation. Again, he may feel identified with the praying guest because he is 'connected' with him by being, for example, his son or friend. Such a connection is, as in pride and shame, enough to involve him in the exposure. Or it may be that he feels embarrassed just because he is a member of the same group, viz., guests at a social gathering, and as such has his share of responsibility to make the evening a success. A guest will remain unembarrassed if he dissociates himself from the group, or if he is a successful member. But the embarrassed guest sees himself as failing to meet the demand imposed on him as a guest.

In the case just described we seem to have an example of someone who does not think of himself as being actually seen or noticed at all and who is embarrassed all the same. It looks as if in his case a reference to an audience is rather pointless as it does not seem to contribute to an explanation of his case. It seems to be rather the demand for a response which is crucial, and not the consciousness of being seen. But this would be a mistaken conclusion to draw: there is after all a link between the demand for a response and being seen. Often at least the demand is created by being seen by eyes other than one's own (under certain circumstances, from a certain point of view). If being seen by other eyes creates the demand then this can come about only if one believes or at least imagines oneself to be actually seen. So here a reference to a seeing audience is in place, and it will be a reference to an audience which is more substantial than that appropriate to shame, for it has to be believed or imagined to be an actual audience. The difficulty about the embarrassed guest was that he did not seem to fit this picture, for his embarrassment was caused not by being seen but by some form of identification.

The identification is, however, with someone who is thought of as being seen. Cases of this type are common enough: a countryman of mine behaves badly (in my view) in front of a foreign audience. I feel embarrassed. Why? He is being seen as a poor specimen, or so I imagine. Because of our shared nationality this verdict affects me as well. But I object to being so seen, so in some way I have to dissociate myself from my countryman, or correct the impression. Here the tension arises not because I actually identify with him, but because I believe that such identification is forced upon me by the audience on the basis of our connection, and so it is up to me to show that such an identification is mistaken. The situation demands that I put matters right ('Englishmen are splendid, really'), but if

I am embarrassed then I cannot see how, or perhaps can see that there is no way of doing so. There is evidently nothing I can do when, for example, I watch my countryman (colleague, member of my family) making a fool of himself in a television interview. In cases such as these being seen still plays an important role and is that which can be said to create the demand for me to respond. But the seeing is an indirect seeing of him who feels the demand. For he is seen only in the sense that the person with whom he is—in his view—seen as identified is being seen, or by him thought to be seen.

The case where a guest is embarrassed because he identifies as a member of a group is parallel to the last one. Because he sees himself as a member of a group of which the praying guest is also a member he is now 'connected' with him. Just as in family relationship, this connection means that he now sees the praying guest's position as affecting his own. The praying guest behaves in a way which is not appropriate guest-behaviour, and is seen to do so. Being seen is here, as in the previous case, the indirect source of the embarrassment. The praying guest is or (the embarrassed guest fears) will shortly become the object of attention and criticism. It is not the fact that he is praying that is embarrassing, just as it was not the fact that I was being useless in an emergency situation which was as such embarrassing to me. If he were discreet about his prayer and prayed quietly to himself while apparently listening to the conversation there would be nothing embarrassing in the situation. The other guest feels embarrassed because his status as a guest has been affected by the behaviour of his fellow guest; he must do something to save his own position, either dissociate himself in some way or raise again the guest status. It is this demand he fails to meet.

There is, then, in embarrassment, an important role for the seeing audience in that directly or indirectly it creates the demand for a response. The status of the audience, viz., its conception as eyes other than my own, is different from its status in shame, and its role is therefore different, too. For if (directly or indirectly) being seen by others is so important here then what is at stake is the agent's appearance to others, or the impression he makes on others, in the given situation. This would, of course, explain why embarrassment, but not shame, is to be regarded as a social emotion, if by this is meant that it is felt in a social context. It presupposes some concern on the part of the agent with the impression he makes on others; somebody who does not care at all how he might be seen by others will not be subject to embarrassment.

The overall demand of the situation is always that he make a certain impression or correct a certain impression which he thinks the audience is left with either because of his own behaviour or because of the behaviour of a member of his group with whom he thinks he will be identified. What is felt in embarrassment is therefore also very different from what is felt in shame. There is here no shock at what is being revealed about oneself, for such revelation is not what is here at issue. What is at issue is the person's inability to respond to what the situation demands. The demand may present itself to him with greater or lesser urgency (one may be mildly or extremely embarrassed) and consequently the tension between the felt demand and the inability to respond may be greater or less. The demand pulls him one way, but there is some obstacle which prevents him from meeting it. The obstacle may be, as in the television case, that there is just nothing that can be done. Or he may be prevented from doing anything by conflicting courses of action presenting themselves to him between which he is unable to decide, or indeed by the demands themselves being seen by him as conflicting.[9] Again, no appropriate response

---

[9] A very nice example of a person being confronted by conflicting demands is provided by Dickens:

> I saw Mr. Guppy, with his hair flattened down upon his head, and woe depicted in his face, looking up at me. . . .
>
> It quite spoilt my pleasure for that night, because it was so very embarrassing and so very ridiculous. But from that time forth, we never went to the play without my seeing Mr. Guppy in the pit . . .
>
> I really cannot express how uneasy this made me. If he would only have brushed up his hair, or turned up his collar, it would have been bad enough; but to know that that absurd figure was always gazing at me . . . put such a constraint upon me that I did not like to laugh at the play, or to cry at it, or to move or to speak. I seemed able to do nothing naturally.' (*Bleak House*, Norton Critical Edition, ed. Ford and Monod, p. 155.)

One natural response for Esther in this situation would be to behave as the admired. But she regards her admirer as absurd, and responding as the admired would make her equally absurd. So this is not a course she can adopt. On the other hand, being gazed at by the absurd Mr. Guppy threatens her position, anyway, so there is a need for her to dissociate herself from him. But Esther can see no way of doing this, and so she remains paralysed in the face of this demand.

may occur to him at all, or, while clear about what ideally he should do he is prevented from embarking on this course of action by, for example, fear of drawing attention to himself or making himself ridiculous. The getting out of one embarrassing situation may only land him in another and possibly worse one.

In embarrassment concern is always with one's own position *vis-à-vis* others. I can feel embarrassed about the impression I think another leaves on the audience only if I think that this will affect the appearance I present. This is one way in which embarrassment may spread to other members of a group.[10] In so far as its concern is always with the agent himself embarrassment is of course like shame, but it is a different kind of concern for it is only with his impression on the given audience. The agent sees himself as failing to respond to whatever it may be the situation requires. But his failure is only relative to the given situation. His embarrassment will be removed by the removal of the demand, and that in turn may be removed either because the situation changes without his doing anything, or by his becoming certain how to respond and acting accordingly. There is no parallel dissolution of the emotion in the case of shame. The reason is of course that when feeling shame his failure is in his own eyes not just relative to the given situation, it is not just a failure to present himself in an appropriate manner to a given audience. In shame the failure is seen as absolute and not as so localized. The self-critical verdict is therefore different in the two cases; in embarrassment it is not an adverse judgement on the person as a whole, but an adverse judgement only on the person in a given situation. It is for this reason that embarrassment is the less undermining of the two emotions.

Shame and embarrassment, then, have each their own sphere of operation. This is not to say, of course, that either may not be the response to the same sort of situation. The man making

---

[10] Goffman seems to think that embarrassment is 'catching' in that the embarrassment of one person in a group may bring about the embarrassment of others because they now feel with or for him (*Interaction and Ritual*, p. 99). This seems to me a mistake, if we are to understand by this claim that these others are now concerned about the position of the initially embarrassed person. Such an explanation seems in any case unnecessary. It is easy enough to see how embarrassment may 'catch on': if in a convention-governed situation the embarrassed person does not play the game other players are now presented with a situation in which the next move is not prescribed so that they, too, may become uncertain about what to do.

the vulgar gesture may have felt embarrassment rather than shame when he noticed an audience, though in that case he would have seen the role of the audience as different, viz., not as just the means towards a new self-recognition, but as that whose view of him needs improving. That either reaction is possible in the same sort of situation is one reason why shame and embarrassment tend not to be disentangled. Another reason is that quite naturally both emotions may be felt at the same time, or the one may be the catalyst for the other. My embarrassment may strike me as showing me up as a lesser person than I hoped I was if the situation is one where I think I should be able to respond naturally and not be paralysed by embarrassment (e.g., the sight of overwhelming grief). Being embarrassed on such an occasion shows up a failing in myself as a human being. Equally, feeling shame may give rise to embarrassment, for finding myself in this paralysing state is bound to affect my response to others. That shame and embarrassment should thus occur together or produce one another is not surprising: how one appears to others and what one is, after all, are not two quite separate elements, and concern with one is likely to be mixed up with or to produce concern with the other. But this consideration does not undermine the validity of their theoretical distinction. In particular it leaves unimpaired the difference in the nature of the respective self-critical judgement, which confirms that in shame more is at stake than how a person presents himself in a social context.

4

At the beginning of this chapter I pointed out that some philosophers speak of different kinds of shame, and pick out only one of these kinds as a moral emotion, in the sense that in this case, but in this case only, feeling shame involves an appeal to some moral standard in the light of which the person is judged, or judges himself. My own claim was that this division into kinds is mistaken, for all cases of shame share the same structure, and what they refer to as 'kinds' are merely specific sets of cases covered by the present analysis. In rejecting the division into kinds I also reject the labelling of just one kind as 'moral'. There is no reason to deny that shame in all its occurrences is a moral emotion, provided that morality is not thought of just in terms of adhering to or breaking certain moral rules, but is taken to include personal morality, a person's own view of how he ought to live and what he ought to be. The final self-directed adverse judgement in shame is always the same: that he is a lesser person than he should be, for an in some way better person would not find himself in a position where he can be seen as he is or may be seen. What is different in the different cases of shame is just that which in the agent's view has made his position so vulnerable. The possible variety here is immense, and, just as in the case of pride, it is impossible to set objective limits to possible objects of shame. Only sometimes is the reason why his position is so vulnerable that he has done something morally disgraceful. To speak of certain cases only as being cases of moral shame is to emphasize the means by which the agent has arrived at the position in which he now finds himself. This is what for instance Rawls has in mind when he says:

Consider first natural shame . . . natural shame is aroused by blemishes in our person, or by acts and attributes indicative thereof . . . Turning now to moral shame . . . someone is liable to moral shame when he prizes as excellences of his person those virtues that his plan of life requires . . . (*A Theory of Justice*, p. 444.)

According to him shame is a moral emotion on those and only those occasions when the agent's explanatory beliefs refer to some failure to act virtuously on his part. But shame may also be thought of as a moral emotion because of the nature of his final self-directed judgement. Rawls himself points to this possibility when he suggests that shame is the feeling someone has when he experiences an injury to his self-respect or suffers a blow to his self-esteem (442). He does not distinguish between self-respect and self-esteem and seems to think that they amount to the same thing (440). But this is not so. They are distinguishable from one another and there is a case for regarding shame as primarily linked with self-respect rather than with self-esteem. They are, however, so interrelated with each other that a neat pigeon-holing of the different phenomena is hardly possible.

The person who has self-esteem takes a favourable view of himself, while he who lacks it will think of himself in unfavourable terms: he is not worth much. If possession and lack of self-esteem consist in these contrasting attitudes a person has towards himself then there is also a third possibility, namely that a person neither possesses nor lacks self-esteem. He has no particular attitude towards himself; he does not give much thought to the matter and takes himself as he comes. There is a connection between self-esteem and emotional pride: the person who is proud of this or that enjoys, at the time of feeling proud, an increase in his self-esteem; he can now take a more favourable view of himself (in some respect). Conversely, a person experiencing shame is forced to think that he is less admirable than he had supposed and this is indeed a blow to his self-esteem. So, as Rawls suggests, shame may well be felt by someone who suffers a blow to his self-esteem. It seems to me, nevertheless, that self-esteem is linked primarily with humiliation rather than with shame, for these two reasons: to suffer a blow to one's self-esteem is to modify one's favourable attitude towards oneself. Hence to suffer such a blow one has to have a favourable attitude towards oneself in the first place. But a person may not have such an attitude. In that case he could not modify it, and so could not experience a blow to his self-esteem, but he could still feel shame under certain circumstances. And secondly, a blow to one's self-esteem may be experienced if the person concerned believes that he does not get the recognition he ought to have, he deserves better than he gets. This is an occasion primarily for humiliation rather than for shame, for he may not therefore also think that he is worth less than he thought.

For a person to have self-respect does not mean that he has a favourable attitude towards himself, or that he has any particular attitude towards himself at all. Nor is self-respect connected with emotional pride. Its connection with pride is different in that the person who respects himself will 'have his pride', he will be too proud to do this or suffer that. Certain kinds of behaviour and certain kinds of treatment will seem intolerable to the person of self-respect, and to pursue or suffer them would mean loss of self-respect to a certain extent. It is true that his expectations concerning his behaviour and treatment may be fulfilled and yet he may not have much self-respect: to respect oneself is to have a sense of one's own value, and this requires also a degree of self-confidence, a belief that he has got his expectations right. But a person who has such confidence in himself and whose relevant expectations are fulfilled need not therefore have a favourable attitude towards himself, for if he thinks of the matter at all he may just think that to behave in such ways or to be so treated is the least a person can expect, and so is not something to be proud of. But while the one does not necessarily lead to the other, it may well be that keeping one's self-respect is often seen as grounds for feeling proud. It has recently been suggested[11] that there is a conceptual connection between self-respect and self-esteem which consists in this: retaining one's self-respect always supplies a ground of reason for self-esteem, and lack or loss of self-respect always supplies a ground for disesteem. This is true, and it is also true that, conversely, retaining one's self-esteem may be a reason for retaining one's self-respect, and loss of self-esteem may involve loss of self-respect. The reason for this is the already familiar point that norms of expectations are pitched at different levels. The implication of this point in the present context is that what people regard as an injury to their self-respect will differ according to what form of behaviour and treatment they expect of and for themselves. Maintaining one's self-respect is then a reason for self-esteem if one thinks that one's norm is a cut above that of others, or that one is better at living up to it than others are. In that case, although in the person's view living up to that norm is only to be expected from a person such as he, it is, against the foil of others, also a reason for self-esteem, or (which comes to the same thing) a reason for being proud of himself. It follows that in such a case not living up to one's norm would at one and the same time be a blow to one's self-esteem and an injury to one's self-respect.

Given these interrelations between self-respect and self-esteem it seems churlish to quarrel with Rawls's view as to what shame is about. But the point is that the occasions for loss of self-respect and the occasions for feeling shame coincide as neither does with the occasion for experiencing a blow to one's self-esteem. The self-respecting person has certain views of what is due to him and from him, though of course these views

---

[11] By David Sachs in *Philosophy and Public Affairs*, Vol. x (1981), pp. 346–60.

may not be very articulate or may formulate themselves only when he is confronted by certain types of action or certain forms of treatment. He will lack self-respect if he has no such views, and he will lose his self-respect if the relevant expectations are not fulfilled. But the frustration of his expectations in this area is precisely the occasion for feeling shame: he will feel shame if he becomes aware that his expectations are being frustrated. This is so because of the nature of these expectations: they relate to the status of the person concerned, and their frustration will, for the agent, amount to a lowering of his status. This is not to say that whenever injury to self-respect then also the experience of shame. For it is conceivable that such injury or loss may not be noticed by the agent. It is the converse which is always true: whenever a person experiences shame then he experiences an injury to his self-respect.

The only possible general point that can be made about the nature of the relevant expectations is that they must be based on something which the agent thinks of great importance, of great value to himself and to the life he envisages himself as leading. What is thought to be of such value will obviously be different for differing agents, and consequently what they see as occasions for shame will differ, too. Some of these values the agent may think of such importance to just his individual life, others he may think are crucial for the life of any human being. But in whatever terms, a person must be able to evaluate himself, his treatment and his actions, if he is to have any self-respect at all.

In the light of this conceptual link between shame and self-respect it does not come as a surprise that we can characterize self-respect by reference to shame: if someone has self-respect then under certain specifiable conditions he will be feeling shame. A person has no self-respect if he regards no circumstances as shame-producing. Loss of self-respect and loss of the capacity for feeling shame go hand in hand. The close connection between these two makes it clear why shame is often thought to be so valuable. It is, firstly, that a sense of value is necessary for self-respect and so for shame, so that whatever else may be wrong about the person feeling shame he will at least have retained a sense of value. And secondly, it is a sense of value which protects the self from what in the agent's own eyes is corruption and ultimately extinction.

The individual member of an honour-group in the setting of a shame-culture can be used to illustrate this point: the relevant values are provided by the honour-code, and his survival as the person he is—which is determined by his membership of the group—depends on his accepting and living by these values. His doing so is therefore protective of the person he is. If on the occasion of his acting against the code he feels shame, then he will at least have retained a sense of what protects that endangered self. He still has some hold on the person he was, so that it is (in theory) still possible for him to regain his old position. But if he feels no shame then he will have abandoned totally the values he lived by, and will have discarded with it the person he once was.[12]

To respect the self, then, is not to think either favourably or unfavourably of the self, but is rather to do that which protects the self from injury or destruction, just as to respect others is not to think well or badly of them, but is at least to abstain from injuring or destroying them, whether physically or morally. And shame is the emotion of self-protection: it may prevent the person concerned from putting himself into a certain position, or make him aware that he ought not to be in the position in which he finds himself. Of course, he may or may not be right in his view of what needs protecting, he may be muddled and misguided in this matter, and so concentrate his energies on protecting a part of himself which is not worth protecting. It is for this reason that in the literature we meet two conflicting views: on the one hand we are told that shame is a good thing,

---

[12] For an example of the importance of shame for members of an honour-group see e.g. Wolfram von Eschenbach's *Parzival* (Translation H. M. Mustard and C. E. Passage). Gurnemanz is advising the young and inexperienced Parzival on the proper conduct of life for one of high birth and breeding:

'Follow *my* advice: it will keep you from wrongdoing. I will begin thus:
    See that you never lose your sense of shame. A man without a sense of shame, what good is he? He lives in a molting state, shedding his honor, and with steps directed towards hell. . . .' (p. 93)

And later, after Parzival has failed in one of his tests, the narrator reassures the reader: 'Still another virtue was his, a sense of shame. Real falsity he had shunned . . .' (p. 172).

and even that it is the supreme virtue;[13] on the other, shame is regarded as an emotion which it is bad to feel, at least on most occasions when it tends to be felt.

The reasons for these opposing views differ, but on the present account the value of shame must lie in its role as self-protective emotion and its disvalue in the possibility of the protection being wholly misplaced. Of course, feelings of shame may be short-lived and non-recurrent if the agent himself recognizes that that which in his view placed him in the vulnerable position should not in fact be seen as bringing about a lowered status.[14] So when in Bunyan's *Pilgrim's Progress* Faithful is told by Shame that few of the powerful and rich would agree with Faithful's view that a tender conscience is a thing of value but would regard it as unmanly, he only briefly accepts the adverse view on a tender conscience and can quickly be made to see that Shame was 'a bold Villain', i.e., be made to recognize that he suffered from false shame. But such recognition may be long delayed or may not happen at all. It is from this point of view that Stanley Cavell discusses the case of Gloucester:

For Gloucester has a fault . . . He has revealed his fault in the opening speeches of the play, in which he tells Kent of his shame. . . . He says that now he is 'braz'd to it', that is, used to admitting that he has fathered a bastard. . . .' He recognizes the moral claim upon himself, as he says twice, to 'acknowledge' his bastard . . . but all this means to him is that he acknowledges that he has a bastard for a son. He does not acknowledge *him*, as a son or a person, with *his* feelings of illegitimacy and being cast out. *That* is something Gloucester ought to be ashamed of; his shame is itself more shameful than his one piece of licentiousness. This is one of the inconveniences of shame, that it is generally inaccurate, attaches to the wrong thing.[15]

As the father of a bastard, Gloucester, in his own view, is in a vulnerable position, for this is an aspect of himself which does

---

[13] Plato in the *Laws* (Bk. 2, 671c) praises shame as that which will prevent a man from doing what is dishonourable. Aristotle in the *Nicomachean Ethics* suggests that while feeling shame is all right for children it is not a suitable emotion for an adult (Bk. 4 Ch. IX), but he also acknowledges its value in *Rhetoric* 1367a10. Both Bollnow (*Die Ehrfurcht*) and Scheler (*Schriften aus dem Nachlass*) emphasize the value of shame.

[14] This is not the only case, of course, where shame may not have much effect. The agent may not think his position so very vulnerable and he may be able to forget with relative ease the occasion for shame.

[15] From 'The Avoidance of Love: A Reading of *King Lear*' in *Must We Mean What We Say?* (CUP, 1976), p. 276.

not fit the sort of person he thinks he ought to be, or wants to be. Revelation of this position (which may be just the recollection that he is in this position) will cause him to experience shame unless he can take certain measures to prevent this occurrence. He takes in fact two steps in this direction. The first (as Cavell later points out) is a very common one under the circumstances: he avoids that which will serve as a reminder to himself and others of what he regards as a flaw in himself, which in this case is achieved by keeping Edmund abroad for long periods of time. The other more daring and interesting move is that he 'brazens it out', that is, he draws attention to the fact that Edmund is illegitimate and so makes it appear that having a bastard son is a less weighty matter than might be supposed. In other words, he tries to turn himself into someone who is shameless: he pretends not to recognize the importance of the value involved and makes light of such a value. Now one may well, like Cavell, believe that Gloucester has got his values all wrong, and that what he should really feel shame about is his treatment of his son, rather than the son's existence. But this of course does not mean that it can be right for Gloucester to make light of his values and thus avoid shame. For in doing so he denies what is in fact of great importance to him. If it were not so important he would not have to take such elaborate steps to avoid exposure. There are therefore two ways of looking at the value of the occurrence of shame in cases like that of Gloucester. The first is Cavell's way in the passage quoted: Gloucester's shame attaches to the wrong object because he has not got his values right. In this sense his shame is misplaced and so unjustified, it is an emotion he ought not to be experiencing. But (and this is the other way of looking at the matter) for the agent it is the experiencing of the emotion which is in this sense justified, and the avoidance of it which is not. Avoidance of shame is one way of losing self-respect, for it is one way of blurring the values the person is committed to. From this point of view genuine shame is always justified, where 'genuine' is to be opposed to the 'false' shame felt by Faithful when for a brief period he let an alien standard be imposed on him. Gloucester, on the contrary, lets an alien standard be imposed on him when he tries to avoid shame, and the one is as much a form of corruption as the other.

Shame can be seen as a moral emotion, then, not because sometimes or even often it is felt when the person believes himself to have done something morally wrong, but rather because the capacity for feeling shame is so closely related to the possession of self-respect and thereby to the agent's values. The implications of this relationship are deeper than has so far been indicated, and can be done justice to only when the notion of integrity has been discussed. First, however, I shall contrast shame with another emotion, namely guilt, which shares with shame the features of being an emotion of self-assessment and of being regarded as a moral emotion, but which in spite of these similarities is quite different in both its structure and its nature.

IV

GUILT AND REMORSE

1

GUILT, unlike shame, is a legal concept. A person is guilty if he breaks a law, which may be of human or divine origin. As a consequence of this action he has put himself into a position where he is liable to punishment, or where, given repentance, he may be forgiven. He will be guilty under these circumstances whether the law is good or bad, pronounced by God or the dictator, backed by good reasons or otherwise. Given only that he is under the legislation of the authority in question, violation of the law is sufficient for guilt.

He may of course *be* guilty and not *feel* guilty, for he may think the law in question bad and oppressive, or he may be quite indifferent towards the authority of the law. To feel guilty he must accept not only that he has done something which is forbidden, he must accept also that it is forbidden, and thereby accept the authority of whoever or whatever forbids it. The person who accepts the authority does not merely recognize its power and so thinks it simply prudent to obey its commands; he also accepts its verdicts as correct and binding. What the authority pronounces to be wrong must not be done. So the authority becomes the voice of conscience. An authority whose commands have to be obeyed has the status of a god, and the notion of the authority of conscience is therefore clearest if it is thought that the voice of conscience reflects the edicts of some god. Otherwise the notion of the authority of conscience remains obscure, though there are of course explanations of how the thought of an authority issuing commands has come to play such an important part in people's lives.[1] The often inarticulate

---

[1] e.g. Freud: 'At the beginning, therefore, what is bad is whatever causes one to be threatened with loss of love. For fear of that loss, one must avoid it . . . A great change takes place only when the authority is internalized through the establishment of a super-ego. The phenomena of conscience then reach a higher stage. Actually, it is not

and obscure notion of an authority plays a role in guilt which is analogous to that played by the notion of an audience in shame: in accepting what he has done as something forbidden the person feeling guilty thinks of himself as being under some authoritative command. He may of course come to question and reject the authority; he may for instance come to discard the religion with which he has grown up. As emotional responses notoriously do not keep step with rationally arrived at decisions he may still feel guilty when, for example, he does not go to church on Sundays. His feelings of guilt would then, in his own view, be irrational. Just as a person is guilty if he breaks the law whether or not that law is just or justified, so he feels guilty if what he does presents itself as a wrong, whether or not what he is doing can in fact be regarded as a wrong, and whether or not he himself thinks it wrong when he views the matter from a more rational point of view. It is for this reason that it is illuminating to describe the person who feels guilty as thinking of himself as having violated some taboo, for this carries the requisite implication of having done something forbidden, without any further indication that what is forbidden is so for good reason because harmful in some respect. Taboos exercise great authority which is often strong enough to survive to some extent and for some time any rational rejection. The categorical imperative is on some level still accepted. Taboos will naturally carry varying degrees of weight, and the struggle to free oneself from them may correspondingly be more or less prolonged. The agent's thought that he has ignored or acted contrary to some categorical imperative, or that he has violated some taboo, must be distinguished from the thought that in doing so he has caused harm to this or that other person. Whether or not he has done so will depend on the content of the command, which may or may not concern the person's behaviour towards others. Guilt, being regarded as a moral emotion, is sometimes thought to be felt essentially about harm done to others. Rawls, for example, thinks that when feeling guilty we think of ourselves as having transgressed what he calls 'a principle of right',[2] so that the

until now that we should speak of conscience or a sense of guilt.' *Civilization and its Discontents* (The Hogarth Press and the Institute of Psycho-Analysis, 1975), pp. 61–2.

[2] *A Theory of Justice*, Part 3, Ch. VII, 67, and Ch. VIII, 72. The 'principle of right' refers to his principles of justice: 'When we go against our sense of justice we explain

wrong I think I have done must be thought of as some harm to another. Here, he thinks, is the difference between feeling guilt and feeling shame, for thinking one has harmed another is not necessary for feeling shame. The distinction sounds plausible enough and fits the cases that easily come to mind: suppose you have not spoken up when you think you should. You will feel shame if your thought is that this just shows what a moral coward you are. But you will feel guilt if you think that because of your keeping quiet justice has not been done. Rawls' own example (445) is of a man who cheats and feels both shame and guilt: he will feel guilt because by wrongly advancing his own interests he has transgressed the rights of others; and he will feel shame because he has shown himself to be unworthy of the trust of his associates. In both these cases feelings of guilt concern themselves with what one has done to others, while feelings of shame concern themselves with one's own standing. And it seems true that guilt does not concern itself with the person's own standing in the way shame does. Nevertheless, the distinction as drawn by Rawls is not quite right. That in feeling guilt I should think of myself as having harmed another applies, perhaps, to the most typical cases, though even here it is not clear that what in my view has been infringed is a principle of right. I may feel guilty because I did not have the patience to listen to somebody's tale of misery, and it seems at least far-fetched to regard this case as falling under some principle of right. On the other hand, it is true that the person who feels guilty thinks in terms of duties not performed and obligations not fulfilled. This is a difference between him and the person feeling shame, who need not think in such terms at all, and is a difference which reference to the transgression of a principle of right no doubt includes. What makes this phrase not wholly suitable as a description of what the guilty think of themselves as having done, is the implied emphasis on persons other than the agent himself. It implies, firstly, that the agent's thoughts are primarily on the rights of others rather than on his own

our feelings of guilt by reference to the principles of justice. . . . The complete moral development has now taken place and for the first time we experience feelings of guilt in the strict sense.' (474.) Rawls is primarily concerned with the mature person's guilt, or guilt in the 'strict' sense; i.e., he has no particular interest in the occurrence of irrational guilt.

duties. Even if every right implies a duty, and the other way about, it may still be the case that the agent thinks of the situation primarily in terms of the one rather than the other. He may look at it from the point of view of how it most importantly concerns himself, or of how it most importantly concerns the other. 'Transgression of a principle of right' fits the latter case rather than the former, but it is the former which applies to the guilty. Nor is it true (as the description is also taken to imply) that he who feels guilty must always think of himself as having harmed another. Principles of right are perhaps too closely linked with the notion of laws governing social behaviour to be invoked entirely appropriately for the case of feeling guilt. If feeling guilty is thought of as the response to having broken such a law then it is naturally thought of as being the response to harm done to others, for to avoid such harm is what these laws are all about. But feelings of guilt need not be so restricted in their scope. I may feel guilty, for example, after a suicide attempt, not because I think that I have caused a lot of trouble to others, but because I think it is just wrong to take life, including my own. Or one may take a Kantian view and think of the deed as an offence against oneself as an autonomous, rational being. Freud cites the case of a man who states that 'the thought plagues me constantly that the guilt is mine for my failure to become what I could have been with my abilities.'[3] Feelings of guilt are often evoked by the thought that one is wasting one's time or abilities. I may feel guilty because I watch that silly television serial rather than improve my mind by reading great literature, but it is hard to see whom under these circumstances I think I harm other than myself. Even if I think devoting myself to serious reading will turn me into a better and wiser person to live with, it may not be for this reason that I feel guilty when I indulge in more frivolous activity. It is not correct, then, that for feeling guilt the thought that directly or indirectly I am harming another must be involved. The crucial thought here is just that what I am doing is forbidden. It is quite natural, of course, that what is so ingrained in us as being forbidden should concern our behaviour towards others, for it is in

[3] Sigmund Freud, 'Determinism, Belief in Chance and Superstition—Some Points of View', in *The Psychopathology of Everyday Life*, ed. J. Strachey (Ernst Benn, London, 1966), p. 244.

this area that early childhood restrictions are most likely to be found, that 'moral training' has its central place. But it is not the only area and hence not what delimits the appropriateness of the guilt-response. What is important for guilt is just that some form of action or abstention should present itself as obligatory to the agent, but the content of the demand is not restricted. In this respect guilt does not differ from shame. In either case it is of course possible that his feelings of guilt or feelings of shame may be judged irrational, but this is not to deny that he feels one or the other of these emotions.

2

In the legal context, to be found guilty is to be found liable to punishment. Guilt and such liability are conceptually connected. Similarly, if a person feels guilty she thinks she has put herself into a position where punishment is due. In acting contrary to the authority's command she has offended that authority and so will expect retribution. This thought must again be distinguished from the thought that some reparation is expected of her. This latter thought connects with the content of the command, rather than with the fact that she has disobeyed it. Consequently, although a common thought in cases of guilt, it is not a feature in all of them. The offence may be thought too great for any form of reparation to be thought possible. There was nothing for Oedipus to repair when he realized that his crimes were those of parricide and incest.

A person is guilty if he has done something which constitutes breaking the law. His guilt is thus localized: given that he has at one time broken one law it does not follow that he has also broken others, or that he will go on breaking the law. What he is punished, or possibly forgiven for is the breaking of whatever is the law in question. Punishment is for what he has done and not for what he is. Both guilt and punishment concentrate on the deed or the omission. Similarly, feelings of guilt are localized in a way in which feelings of shame are not localized; they concern themselves with the wrong done, not with the kind of person one thinks one is. This difference is brought out quite well by a distinction drawn by some sociologists between 'primary' and 'secondary' deviance.[4] 'Primary deviance' applies to those cases where a person accepts that he has done wrong but does not think of this wrong-doing as affecting his overall standing as a person. What he has done remains, in his own view, alien to what he really is. The secondary deviant, however, now sees himself not just as a man who at some point, for instance, committed a burglary, but rather sees himself as a burglar. What he has done is not alien to himself but on the contrary expresses what he really is. This second view is appropriate to shame, the former to guilt—though of course neither feeling is a necessary consequence of taking the relevant view, for in either case the individual may remain indifferent or become reconciled to the state of affairs.

If feelings of guilt concentrate on the deed or the omission then the thought that some repayment is due is in place here as it is not in the case of shame. If I have done wrong then there is some way in which I can 'make up' for it, if only by suffering punishment. But how can I possibly make up for what I now see I am? There are no steps that suggest themselves here. There is nothing to be done, and it is best to withdraw and not to be seen. This is the typical reaction when feeling shame. Neither punishment nor forgiveness can here perform a function.

If repayment and punishment are appropriate to guilt but not to shame, then it is natural to assume that guilt is related to responsibility in a way in which shame is not. Normally we are held responsible for what we do in a way in which we are not held responsible for what we are. What we do or fail to do can be set against a background which may at least mitigate the guilt by pleas of ignorance, lack of intention or unfortunate circumstances. Excuses of this sort are irrelevant in the case of shame, for the occasion of shame may be something one could not conceivably do anything about, such as having poor parents or growing old. Similarly, one would suppose, feelings of guilt but not feelings of shame are based on the agent's thinking himself responsible for what he has done. It is indeed true to say that when feeling guilty but not when feeling shame I must

---

[4] e.g. Edwin Lemert, 'Primary and Secondary Deviation' (1951), in Cressey and Ward, *Delinquency, Crime and Social Process* (Harper and Row, N.Y., 1969). I am grateful to Jeremy Waldron for drawing my attention to this literature.

think myself responsible for the relevant state of affairs, but this is true only given the widest possible reading of 'responsibility'. I may but need not think of myself as having intentionally or negligently done or omitted to do what I feel guilty about; I may but need not think that I could and should have acted otherwise and so am blameworthy in the accepted sense. Normally, perhaps, I do think myself blameworthy in this sense when feeling guilty, but not necessarily so: while driving my car I knock down and kill a child whom I could not have seen or, once seen, have avoided. I have not been negligent but have taken all possible care, and I know that this is the case. But I have done a terrible thing, and my seeing it as such is enough for me to suffer from guilt. It is of course possible that although I know I have not been negligent I do not quite believe it, and so after all think myself negligent and therefore blameworthy. But this is not the only possible explanation. However little I could have helped the accident, nevertheless I brought it about. In this minimal sense of 'responsible' I am responsible for it. Responsibility of this sort was quite sufficient for the self-condemnation of Oedipus: he had violated the taboos of parricide and incest, and ignorance of what he was doing is quite irrelevant to his feelings of guilt. Causal responsibility is the type that is sufficient for guilt, and that much is also necessary. If I feel guilty about my privileged position in society due to circumstances of birth then I see myself as an agent causally involved: it is *my* birth which has brought about the state of affairs which is my privileged position. The case is quite different if I feel shame about the circumstances of my birth: my agency or otherwise is here irrelevant, it is enough that I think of it as in some way deflating my status. This difference between these two emotions is illustrated by the fact that the deed of another (my child, my compatriot) may make me feel shame but not guilt. Guilt itself cannot be vicarious,[5] and feelings of guilt similarly cannot arise from the deeds or omissions of others. The relationship between myself and, for example, my children is enough for their misdeeds or failures to cause me shame, but it is not enough to cause me feelings of guilt. My son's misdeeds may by me be taken to show my own failure as a parent, but

[5] Cp. Joel Feinberg, *Doing and Deserving* (OUP, 1970), Ch. IX, p. 231.

I am not causally responsible for these particular deeds. His own agency has broken whatever causal chain there may be between his defective upbringing and his present behaviour. So I cannot feel guilty about his particular behaviour on this occasion, though I may, of course, feel guilty about my own treatment of and attitude towards him which, in my view, may have contributed to making him the sort of person he now is. It is therefore true that, as one would expect, responsibility, like punishment, is essentially linked with guilt and not with shame. It is because of the agent's thought that he is directly instrumental in bringing about some forbidden state of affairs that he thinks of himself as 'owing payment', as being liable to retribution. But this is a thought which is irrelevant to him who feels shame.

It is also because he thinks himself responsible in this sense that we can account for the effect the deed or state of affairs has on him. The thought involved here is not so much: 'I have done this terrible thing *to him*;' but is rather: '*I* have done this terrible thing to him.' Guilt is a burden he has to carry, he cannot disown it, it must leave its mark upon him. Earlier I suggested as appropriate to the person who feels guilty that he regard what he has brought about as somehow alien to himself, as not being part of what he really is. If he feels guilty about his privileged position then he sees this as the stain on, say, an otherwise admirable communist. It mars but does not destroy the whole. If, on the other hand, he feels shame about his privileged position then he thinks of it as threatening his status as a communist altogether. Similarly, if I feel guilty about my wasted life then I think I have failed to make use of the gifts and capacities I possess, I have not developed what I really am but have led a life that is alien to the 'real' me. But if I feel shame about the way I have lived my life then I see it as being just the sort of life a person of my sort would lead; neither is worth very much. When feeling guilty, therefore, the view I take of myself is entirely different from the view I take of myself when feeling shame: in the latter case I see myself as being all of a piece, what I have just done, I now see, fits only too well what I really am. But when feeling guilty I think of myself as having brought about a forbidden state of affairs and thereby in this respect disfigured a self which otherwise remains the same.

3

It is because the agent at the time of feeling guilt thinks of himself as the person (causally) responsible for the relevant state of affairs that he sees the disfigurement in himself as brought about by himself. So, if at all possible, he should do something about it. He cannot wipe it out, for what is done is done. But by paying in some way he can make up for it. One form the payment may take is that he accepts retribution. It is from this debit and credit point of view that the notion of punishment as restoring the balance makes its point. Whatever one may think of the virtues and defects of the theory that punishment is a means of restoring the balance, of making it possible for the individual to retake his place in society, this notion of punishment or repayment is essential to the guilty person's view of the situation. There are naturally degrees of feeling guilt, and the thought that he owes payment may on many occasions not be particularly persuasive or lasting. He may manage to live with himself quite happily and to regard the disfigurement as minor enough to be ignored. In serious cases, however, it cannot be ignored, and in such circumstances there are roughly three options available to him who suffers from guilt.

i. Firstly, he may make repayment as best he can and regard the matter as closed.
ii. Secondly, perhaps not thinking the first solution within his reach, he may adjust himself to the alteration in himself by now continuing in a way consistent with it, by making the disfigurement disappear by disfiguring himself still further.
iii. Finally, he may just continue to suffer the guilt with possibly serious consequences to himself.

The first solution can take different forms. The 'repayment' may consist in just accepting whatever the punishment may be, or it may consist in a more positive attempt on the agent's part to repair the damage his action may have caused to others. Either way, but particularly in the second case, this solution is the most straightforward and the best for all concerned. It is socially acceptable as the person concerned will have made amends, and is satisfactory for the person himself as he will have rid himself of an unpleasant and possibly destructive state. The other options may lead to total wickedness or madness respectively.

Macbeth affords a clear example of a case fitting the second solution: he sees his first murder, that of Duncan, as leaving a terrible stain upon him. Immediately after the murder he cannot say 'amen'. 'But wherefore could I not say "amen"?' he asks, and adds ' "Amen" stuck in my throat.' Lady Macbeth, at this point intensely practical, warns him:

> These deeds must not be thought
> After these ways: so, it will make us mad.   (II. ii.)

Macbeth eventually takes her advice and remains quite sane. He acclimatizes himself to the alteration within him by behaving in ways which makes the alteration no longer appear as something alien to the person he is, but makes it appear rather as the norm: driven by overriding ambition, going in for murder is just what Macbeth does. In acting as he does he avoids the threat of shame. When we first meet him he is still a man of honour who takes seriously the relevant code which prescribes how a king and guest ought, or at any rate ought not, to be treated:

> . . . He's here in double trust:
> First, as I am his kinsman and his subject,
> Strong both against the deed; then, as his host . . .   (I. vii.)

As a man of honour he must see the murder of his king and guest as disgraceful. But once he has done the deed he changes his point of view. Ignoring obligations to king and guest is part of the man who ruthlessly pursues his aim. From this new point of view it is not the murder he sees as degrading; it is rather the giving up of his ambition which would be cowardly and weak. During his initial period of doubt Lady Macbeth treats him as a moral coward and turns the murder of Duncan into a test of courage:

> . . . Art thou afeard
> To be the same in thine own act and valour
> As thou art in desire? Would'st thou have that
> Which thou esteem'st the ornament of life,

And live a coward in thine own esteem,
Letting 'I dare not' wait upon 'I would',
Like the poor cat i' th'adage?'   (I. vii.)

The ploy works. What Macbeth now sees as the shameful
course is the giving up of his ambition; to abstain from murder-
ing Duncan would be weakness and failure. So he now lives by
a new code according to which 'honour' consists in ruthlessly
pursuing one's aim at whatever cost to those who happen to be
in the way. Bradley has a point when he says that the murder of
Duncan is done, 'one may almost say, as if it were an appalling
duty'.[6] In a perverted way Macbeth is trying to maintain his
integrity.

Lady Macbeth herself is an example fitting the last of the
three possibilities given: she is unable to follow her own advice
and comes to see her part in the murder as a disfigurement of
herself she cannot live with. She was wrong when initially she
believed a little water would be enough to clean her. She obsess-
ively washes her hands, but no amount of washing will get rid
of the blood. So she suffers the fate she herself predicts for those
in her position and goes mad. In her madness she tries to dissociate herself from that part of herself that was accomplice to a
murder. What one cannot live with one has to get rid of. Lady
Macbeth pursues this course consistently enough by finally
committing suicide. Dissociation is a feature of unbearable
guilt (normally restricted to cases of murder), and is a consequence of the agent's view that the doer of the terrible deed is
alien to his real self. In literature it is therefore not uncommon
for the murderer to experience himself as being somehow two
selves. Jonas, in Dickens's *Martin Chuzzlewit*, for example, has
just murdered a blackmailer and is now on his way home. He is
terrified of entering his room. He is supposed to have been in
his room all the time while in fact he was otherwise engaged.
He knows perfectly well, of course, that at the moment he is on
his way to London and not in his own room at all. But it seems
as if he had left the 'good' self behind while the 'bad' self went
about its business. He sees himself 'as it were, a part of the
room', and he is afraid not so much *for* himself as *of* himself.
Dickens says of him that 'he became in a manner his own ghost

---

[6] A. C. Bradley, *Shakespeare Tragedy* (Macmillan, 1929), Lecture 9, p. 358.

and phantom, and was at once the haunting spirit and the haunted man.'[7]

Macbeth, with his perverted integrity, also and consequently perverts the dissociation: he does not try and dissociate himself from the doer of the terrible deed for this is now not what he sees as alien. He dissociates himself rather from the good and honourable. His murder of Banquo, under whom 'his genius is rebuk'd', would then be seen as Macbeth killing what represents the better side of his nature.

The split experienced in such extreme cases of guilt is comprehensible in the light of the two features mentioned earlier: the agent has brought about something which is yet alien to himself. If he can neither restore himself to his unblemished self nor adjust himself to the altered one, then there seems no alternative for him but to see himself as two distinguishable selves. No doubt some compromise is possible, as psychoanalytic theory suggests: he may conceal from himself the kind of disfigurement it is and persuade himself that it is of a nature which, though bad enough is at least bearable to live with. In 'Dostoevsky and Parricide', Freud suggests that Dostoevsky's feelings of guilt arose from his wish to kill his father. 'As often happens with neurotics, Dostoevsky's burden of guilt had taken tangible shape as a burden of debt.' On this view, Dostoevsky sees his guilt as relating to his gambling whereas it in fact relates to his thoughts about his father. It goes without saying that being an obsessive gambler is better at any rate than being a parricide. One need not accept the whole of that theory to agree that it is plausible that some such replacement should sometimes occur. Equally plausible in the light of the need of the guilty to dissociate themselves from the doer of the deed is Auden's theory about the function of the detective story.[8] The

---

[7] Charles Dickens, *Martin Chuzzlewit*, Ch. XLVII. Richard III takes a similar view of himself when, on the eve of the battle of Bosworth, the ghosts of all those for whose deaths he is responsible appear to him:

> What do I fear? Myself? There's none else by.
> Richard loves Richard; that is, I am I.
> Is there a murderer here? No. Yes. I am. . . .
> All several sins . . .
> Throng to the bar, crying all guilty! guilty!   (V. iii. 182–99.)

[8] W. H. Auden, 'The Guilty Vicarage', in *The Dyer's Hand* (Faber & Faber, 1975), p. 158.

detective story, needless to say, is escape literature, and the fantasy it allows the reader to indulge in is that guilt in the shape of the murderer is uncovered in someone other than himself, thereby proving his innocence.

The magic formula is an innocence which is discovered to contain guilt; then a suspicion of being the guilty one; and finally a real innocence from which the guilty other has been expelled, a cure effected, not by me or my neighbors, but by the miraculous intervention of a genius from outside who removes guilt by giving knowledge of guilt. (The detective story subscribes, in fact, to the Socratic daydream: 'Sin is ignorance'.)

The satisfaction the detective story therefore provides is the illusion of being dissociated from the murderer, and so it is suitable, perhaps addictive, reading for those who suffer from a sense of sin. No such possibility of escape is provided for those who are prey to recurrent feelings of shame. Dissociation from, or repression of, the alien doer of the deed is not here available precisely because the doer of the deed is not seen as alien but on the contrary as bringing out into the open what the agent really is. For the same reason it is impossible for the person who feels shame to do as Macbeth does and alter himself in such a way that the doer of the deed is no longer alien; all he can do in this respect is to revise his picture of himself and try to reconcile himself to that.

4

If feeling guilty involved no more than the thought that the agent had harmed another then there would be no reason to regard guilt as an emotion of self-assessment. But this is the class of emotions to which it belongs. From this point of view it is quite different from remorse, an emotion with which it is often linked under the heading 'moral emotions'. The important feature of guilt is that the thought of the guilty concentrates on herself as the doer of the deed. Having brought about what is forbidden she has harmed herself. She has put herself into a position where repayment from her is due, but the point of the payment is not, or is only incidentally, that a moral wrong should be righted. This, the righting of a moral wrong, may well be the form the repayment takes, but from the point of view of the guilty person this is only a means towards the end: that she should be rid of the burden, that she should be able again to live with herself. The painfulness of the guilt-feelings is therefore explained as the uneasiness the person concerned feels about herself. That they so often express themselves as a worry about how to put right an injustice done to others is natural but not essential to the case; it is due to the fact that so often what we regard as the wrong done is an action harming others, so that repairing the harm is necessary to restore the balance. That, in the agent's view, reparation is required is due to her conception of herself as disfigured and the consequent need to do something about it. The greater the supposed disfigurement the greater, of course, such a need—and the more unlikely, perhaps, that the agent should think adequate payment is possible. Hence the self-torments the guilty sometimes let themselves in for.

The thought in remorse, by contrast, concentrates on the deed rather than on the agent as he who has done the deed. Remorse, the *OED* tells us, is a feeling of compunction, or deep regret, for a sin or wrong committed. This is acceptable in so far as it brings out one way in which remorse differs from regret: remorse is felt about a sin or moral wrong whereas regret is felt about what is in some way undesirable, but not particularly morally so. But it would be a mistake to conclude that remorse is regret which operates over a narrower, viz., moral, area. The two emotions differ also in other central respects.[9] Regret but not remorse can be felt about an event for which the agent does not take herself to be even just causally responsible. I may regret the passing of the summer; Hamlet regretted that circumstances had forced him into a position where he had to act against his own nature. He could not, seeing the situation in this way, have felt remorse. Remorse is always felt about an event which the agent sees as an action of hers. It is therefore not surprising that the person who feels remorse and the person who feels regret should view differently the relevant past event. If she feels remorse then she wants to

---

[9] For a more detailed discussion of some of these points see Amélie Rorty, 'Agent-Regret', *Explaining Emotions*, pp. 489–506. The Hamlet example is hers.

undo the action and its consequences which cause the remorse, but when feeling regret she need not think that she would undo the action if she could. She may regret an action (sacking an employee) which overall she still considers necessary and beneficial (as leading to the more productive employment of labour). It is possible also to regret an action but accept it as the thing to do under the same description: she regrets sacking the employee because the girl was so easily crushed, but she had to be sacked, nevertheless, because she was so inefficient. Perhaps regret always implies acceptance of what has been done. It had to be done although there were unfortunate or disagreeable aspects to the deed. Remorse, on the other hand, never implies acceptance. It is impossible to feel remorse and yet believe that overall it was right to act as one did. The aspect of the action which causes remorse, or the description under which the remorseful agent sees her action, is regarded by her as outweighing any possible good that may have come of it. Agamemnon, for example, whatever else he may have felt about having caused his daughter to be sacrificed, could not have felt remorse about his action while continuing to think that her sacrifice was necessary for the Greek fleet to be able to sail, and that this was the overriding good. He could have felt regret, though unless this is qualified (deep, bitter) it would seem a rather inadequate reaction under the circumstances.

These differences between the emotions are reflected in their respective connection with action. No action need follow from regret, or even need be expected to follow. This is not surprising if the agent may think that all things considered she did the right thing, or did what had to be done. But we do expect some sort of action from her who feels remorse, though of course we may expect in vain. She wants to undo what she has done, and although it is evidently impossible to do just that, she would normally be expected to try and do something towards repairing the damage she takes herself to have brought about. If she takes no such steps the claim that she feels remorse would be suspect.

The person feeling remorse is tied to her action as the person feeling regret is not. She must do something about it, or it will continue to worry her. But at the same time there is a sense in which she remains detached as she cannot do when feeling either guilt or shame. Remorse is not an emotion of self-assessment, the concentration of thought is here not on the self, on its disfigurement or lowly standing, but is on her actions and their consequences. It is more outward-looking than either of the other two. Guilt and remorse may be experienced about the same event. Macbeth initially feels remorse as well as guilt, he wishes the deed could be undone: 'Wake Duncan with thy knocking: I wish thou could'st.' This is different from his guilt-reaction; his inability to say 'amen' indicates that he is now marked as an outsider who has broken his relationship with God. As the beliefs involved in the emotions are different, it is equally possible to feel the one but not the other. While Agamemnon could not have felt remorse under the circumstances I have described, he could have felt guilt, for that an action is thought to be necessary under given circumstances does not interfere with the adverse effect which having done the deed may have on the agent. Jonas, while burdened with guilt, feels no remorse at all, for he does not wish to be back in the situation where he was plagued by a blackmailer:

Still he was not sorry. No. He had hated the man too much, and had been bent, too desperately and too long, on setting himself free. If the thing could have come over again, he would have done it again . . . . There was no more penitence or remorse within him now than there had been while the deed was brewing.

(*Martin Chuzzlewit*, Ch. XLVII.)

It is equally possible that a person should experience remorse but not guilt, where the agent does not see herself burdened or stained by her wrongdoing. The wrong done need not present itself to her who feels remorse as forbidden, she need not think of herself as having disobeyed a categoric demand. Not every action a person sees as morally undesirable and would like to undo need be seen by her as leaving a stain.[10]

Remorse, guilt, and shame are usually classed together as 'moral emotions'. But remorse seems to be 'moral' in a sense

---

[10] Jane Austen's Emma Woodhouse, after the disastrous party on Boxhill, feels humiliated and remorseful, but she feels no guilt. She thinks of herself as being perfect in her behaviour to others, and it is humiliating to be shown that sometimes she is nothing of the sort. But she is also kind and feels sorry to have hurt Miss Bates's feelings. In order to undo the harm she has done she is prepared to undergo the tedium of a morning visit. She does not think of herself as having neglected a duty or left an obligation unfulfilled, but she thinks of herself as having failed to live up to the standards she has set for herself.

in which neither of the others is. Shame, I suggested, may suitably be labelled a 'moral emotion' because of its connection with self-respect, but what a particular agent considers necessary to retain his self-respect may itself not be moral at all. It may be morally irrelevant as when, for example, he regards some physical defect as a threat to his self-respect. Or it may itself be morally wrong, as would presumably be some of the expectations which the arrogant or conceited need to see fulfilled if the basis for their self-respect is not to be undermined. In the case of the guilty, the content of what the agent sees as forbidden or obligatory can hardly seem morally irrelevant, at least to him. But it need not be the case that what he sees in these terms is in fact wrong or evil. In particular, neither of these emotions is moral in the sense of being other-regarding, for the agent's chief concern is for himself. Remorse, on the other hand, seems to be moral in just this sense; though perhaps not necessarily, at least standardly the agent is here concerned with the effect of what he does on others. As it concentrates on the action rather than the actor it also seems the healthier emotion, for in turning the agent away from himself he is less threatened by the possibility of self-preoccupation and self-indulgence.

Sometimes remorse is thought to be of value for the additional reason, that it is only through remorse that the guilty can be redeemed, so that remorse is the means whereby the guilty can regain his former position. The Bible emphasizes that repentance is necessary for God's forgiveness, and it may be that analogously in a non-Christian context remorse is necessary for the guilty to be re-established. This is the view held by Scheler. He regards remorse as the emotion of salvation. On his theory guilt and remorse are related to each other as 'promptings of conscience'. Guilt, it seems, is potentially merely destructive: the man who feels guilty recognizes that he has acted against his conscience, and this recognition will not let him rest and will create a tension within himself. Such torments are in themselves sterile. On the other hand, recognition of guilt is a necessary first step towards salvation; if a person ignores his wrongdoing then we have a case of 'hardening of heart' and nothing fruitful can come of that. It is in remorse that the agent takes a positive attitude towards the situation and himself. It constitutes a 'change of heart', or a totally new attitude, and through it the agent can regain his powers and rebuild himself. Scheler therefore does not stress so much that remorse is outgoing and other-regarding, but sees it rather as that which heals the self and enables it to lead a new life.[11] This does not mean, however, that on this view the thoughts involved in remorse must concentrate on the self, that remorse, too, is an emotion of self-assessment. The healing-process of the self may on the contrary be possible only if the agent looks outward at the world, rather than inward at himself.

On Scheler's view remorse is wholly constructive and guilt is merely destructive. He has made this true by definition: whatever is destructive in the person's attitude and behaviour counts as guilt; whatever constructive counts as remorse. Both points are debatable. There are possible cases of remorse where that emotion seems as destructive and possibly self-indulgent as guilt may be. Far from prompting repair work and bringing about a new and hopeful attitude towards the future, it may just torment the sufferer. A person can make the most of remorse by insisting on seeing what he has done under a description which strikes him as unalterable. A dutiful niece may, after the death of her aunt, feel remorse not because she did not give her the time and care that were needed, but because she did not do so for the right reasons. At the time it suited her to live with her aunt and look after her although her affections were not particularly engaged. What she wants to but cannot undo is her behaviour under the description 'suiting my own purposes' and substitute for it 'devoting myself lovingly and unselfishly to my aunt'. So remorse continues to gnaw at her. Nor does it seem to be the case that, conversely, guilt must always be destructive. In the following quotation Melanie Klein puts a different view:

The irrevocable fact that none of us is ever entirely free from guilt has very valuable aspects because it implies the never fully exhausted wish to make reparation and to create in whatever way we can. All social services benefit by this urge. In extreme cases, feelings of guilt

[11] Max Scheler, 'Reue und Wiedergeburt', in: *Vom Ewigen im Menschen, Ges. Werke*, Band V (Bern, 1954). He describes remorse as from the moral point of view 'eine Form der Selbstheilung der Seele', and as from the religious point of view 'der natürliche Akt, den Gott der Seele verlieh, um zu Ihm zurückzukehren.' (p. 33.)

drive people towards sacrificing themselves completely to a cause or to their fellow beings, and may lead to fanaticism . . . ('Our Adult World and its Roots in Infancy', Tavistock Publications, 1959.)

Scheler's view seems too extreme. It is a more plausible suggestion that, rather than being in this respect so sharply contrasted, both guilt and remorse may be either constructive or destructive, depending on the agent and his view of the situation. There is always the possibility of this view being distorted; like shame, or indeed like any emotion, remorse may be wrongly directed and quite irrational. Feeling remorse no doubt has its value, but this does not mean that it must always be constructive.

But while not acceptable as it stands, Scheler's view nevertheless directs attention to the way in which guilt and remorse both differ from and are related to each other. Earlier I distinguished features which are essential to feeling guilt from those which may quite understandably but still mistakenly be taken to be essential. The person feeling guilt believes that she has done something forbidden and that in doing what is forbidden she has disfigured and so harmed herself. This is the identificatory belief. She may or may not also believe that what she did was harmful to either others or herself. The first, essential, type of harm is the direct consequence of the deed being forbidden; the second, non-essential type of harm is contingent on the nature of whatever it may be the agent sees as forbidden. That may be, for instance, violating another's rights, or it may be neglecting her talents. In the latter case, therefore, the person is harmed under two descriptions, that she has done what is wrong, and that she has not developed her talents. In this case doing the latter also happens to constitute the former, but the specific way in which she thinks she has harmed herself is distinguishable from the harm that is the stain of guilt. Secondly and consequentially, it is central to guilt that the agent sees herself in a position where repayment is due, but not that she thinks she must repair and so in some way undo the damage she has caused. This may or may not be the form in which she thinks she might be able to make up for what she has done.

The two features just rejected as being not essential to guilt are so partly because they need not be present in all cases of it.

But even where the person feeling guilt believes that she has harmed another and believes that she should now repair this damage, her thoughts are not primarily on this aspect of the situation, they are primarily on herself. In this sense, too, the thought of damage caused and so to be repaired is inessential. In feeling remorse, on the other hand, it is precisely these thoughts which are the agent's identificatory beliefs, i.e., when feeling remorse the agent believes that she has done harm which she ought to try and repair.

This account agrees with Scheler's in so far as remorse is also constructive. It differs from Scheler's in that guilt need not be wholly destructive; it will be constructive on those occasions when the person feeling guilty believes that repairing the damage is the form her repayment should take. But she, unlike the person feeling remorse, will not regard her repair work as an end in itself. She will see it rather as a means towards self-rehabilitation. There are therefore occasions when the person feeling guilt may do or think she ought to do exactly the same as the person feeling remorse, and it may be impossible for anyone, including the person concerned, to tell whether she is prompted by feelings of guilt or by remorse.

Remorse, though being constructive in that it implies the view that repair-work is due, need not therefore be constructive on all relevant occasions. The remorseful niece is a case in point. But what she feels seems to be a mixture of both guilt and remorse. In so far as she thinks that she has done damage which she ought to do something about, she feels remorse. But as the damage is caused by the (in her view) non-altruistic reasons for action rather than by her actual behaviour her thoughts also concentrate on the disfigurement of herself as a moral agent, and so there are also guilt feelings. That there can be such hybrid cases is explained by the possibility of a partial overlap of the beliefs involved in these two emotions.

Remorse may be constructive and yet not other-regarding: the repair work the agent thinks should be done may be to mend the damage she has caused herself. This seems at least a possibility; wasting one's talents, spoiling one's chances in life through drug-taking or alcohol may well be a matter for remorse. On the other hand, as the identificatory belief is not directly about the self, remorse, unlike guilt and shame is at least a candidate for other-regarding thought and behaviour. It is, perhaps rightly, thought to be in practice standardly other-regarding. If this is correct, then the reason may be that where a person has caused harm to herself of a nature which can prompt remorse rather than regret, then the harm is likely to be sufficiently serious to concentrate her thought on herself to the exclusion of other possible objects. The person would then in such circumstances be more likely to feel guilt rather than remorse. But whether or not this is so, it is clear that here is a basis for regarding remorse as a 'moral' emotion which is totally lacking in shame and guilt.

On Scheler's account remorse presupposes guilt, for the role of remorse is specifically to heal and re-establish the guilty. While it seemed wrong to restrict the operation of remorse in this way (a person may feel remorse about something he has done and feel no guilt), where the two are linked Scheler's emphasis on the constructiveness of remorse may have a significance not yet allowed for. The point concerns forgiveness. The agent who feels guilty believes that through his wrongdoing he has spoilt his relationship with the god disobeyed or the person harmed. The recipient of the wrong (provided he shares this view of the situation) is now in a position where he may either forgive or withhold forgiveness. For him to forgive is for him to recognize the wrong done to him but to re-accept the agent in spite of it, to re-establish the relationship. But if he so re-establishes the relationship without there being a 'change of heart' on the agent's part then it seems it is not genuine forgiveness he offers, but condonation.[12] For in re-accepting the unrepentant agent he would seem to think little of the wrong done and so compromise his own values. If so, then to be genuinely forgiven and thereby to be re-established in the previous relationship the agent must be sincere in wishing the deed undone, he must, it seems, feel remorse. Nor is the need for remorse restricted to this case: it may be that the agent, if he is to live with himself again, will have to forgive himself, and if genuine forgiveness must be preceded by remorse, then remorse is required on all such occasions as well. Kolnai, in his paper

---

[12] For a discussion of condoning versus forgiving see Aurel Kolnai, 'Forgiveness', in *Proceedings of the Aristotelean Society*, 1973–4. Kolnai concedes, somewhat grudgingly, that remorse is not necessarily required for genuine forgiveness.

on 'Forgiveness', suggests that forgiveness granted to ourselves is a fairly dubious concept, 'if only because a person cannot "wrong" himself, i.e. infringe his own rights' (106). Kolnai, like Rawls, connects guilt with principles of right, and this itself seemed dubious. It is, however, not this point that matters here. If it is true that forgiveness is necessary to restore a spoilt relationship then the agent himself will have to forgive himself, for *qua* doer of the relevant deed he has alienated himself from himself, and this would seem to be the most important relationship of all to restore. So in all (serious) cases of guilt, for the person concerned to re-establish himself, to regard himself again as a whole and so to live at peace with himself, self-forgiveness is necessary. 'You must learn to forgive yourself' seems in such circumstances very sensible advice. And if genuine forgiveness requires remorse, then so will self-forgiveness. On this view of forgiveness it is true that, as Scheler says, remorse has a very specific constructive function.

The view that genuine forgiveness requires remorse is too extreme to be acceptable as it stands. Whether forgiveness of a wrong is genuine or is a case of condonation will depend on the circumstances of individual cases. It seems quite possible for a generous person to forgive a wrongdoer who does not show much sign of a change of heart without thereby being indifferent to whatever wrong he may have committed. Whether forgiveness in these circumstances is wise or foolish is of course a different question. But in the case of self-forgiveness such generosity would hardly be in place; it would suspiciously look like being indulgent towards oneself and making matters too easy for oneself. Maybe in the case of self-forgiveness such charity is always a form of condonation, and if so remorse retains something of the importance Scheler ascribes to it. It would remain at least one means of reconciling the agent to himself.[13]

[13] But not, I think, the only means. e.g. in the last chapter of *Crime and Punishment* Dostoevsky hints at a heading process which is differently based: Raskolnikoff, now a prisoner in Siberia, does not feel remorse. 'He did not repent of his deeds', he merely thought he had made mistakes, and in particular that he had been feeble to confess. Yet there is a change in his attitude, the beginning of a healing process: 'They were both worn and ill, but in those white and worn faces already beamed the dawn of a restored future, and full resurrection to a new life.' His fellow-convicts begin to look kindly upon him, for the first time he is accepted. But this renewal is due not to remorse but to love.

Remorse was initially introduced to provide a contrast to guilt, and to the emotions of self-assessment in general. As a moral emotion it has in common with guilt and shame only the feature that it requires a sense of value on the part of the agent, an awareness, more or less developed, of moral distinctions, of what is right or wrong, honourable or disgraceful. In other respects it differs from them just because it is not an emotion of self-assessment. In feeling remorse a person's thoughts are not primarily upon himself, it is not the agent himself who occupies the centre of the stage. He is not seen by some audience, nor judged by some authority. The person who feels remorse sees himself as a responsible moral agent, and so sees whatever wrong he has done as an action (or omission) of his about the consequences of which he ought, if possible, to do something. Both guilt and shame are more passive by comparison. In neither of these cases need the person concerned see the occasion for the emotion as an action of his. Shame is passive also in that it leaves the agent helpless. In guilt, the thought that by having done what is forbidden he is now in a position where punishment or forgiveness is appropriate gives him initially the passive role of a possible recipient of the actions of another, rather than that of an active agent. And he may not conceive of himself as a possible active agent at all, for he may be resigned to the view that he who violates a taboo just has to accept whatever retribution is due to him. In so far as the perceived stain on the self gives him a motive for repair work it is only incidental if it is of the same sort as that prompted by remorse.

V

INTEGRITY

THE thoughts which are constitutive of the emotions of self-assessment are directed towards the self and its status. A person, to be able to experience these emotions, needs a form of self-consciousness which is not just the capacity to ascribe experiences to himself, though this is of course a minimum requirement. The person concerned must be capable of being self-conscious also in the sense that he can see himself as a being that can be seen by others, that can be assessed and judged.

If there is self-consciousness there is a self to be conscious of. This does not imply that there is one unchanging entity, the self, which is the object of such consciousness. The self is not unchanging, and it cannot be the object of consciousness in the way in which a physical object or event can be an object of consciousness. The 'perceiver' is part of that self and so contributes to what it is. He can affect and shape what he perceives as the observer of the physical event cannot affect and shape what he perceives.

The person capable of experiencing the emotions of self-assessment sees himself from the point of view of being an agent in the world, who tries and succeeds or fails to bring about certain states of affairs; he sees himself as affected by others, and he takes a view of his own effectiveness and the value of what he has achieved. He sees himself as a moral agent, at least in the minimal sense that he thinks about himself and his life evaluatively. As such an agent he has an identity. Necessarily, the identity of the moral agent depends on other criteria for self-identity being fulfilled; in particular, for it to be possible for an agent to assess himself, there must be a degree of connectedness between his states of consciousness. But the dependence is one way only: a being's identity as moral agent may be lost without this affecting any identity he may have in mental or physical terms.[1] The problem concerning the identity of a moral agent is not how to re-identify the same individual in different situations; this point is assumed to be settled. It is rather the question of what identifies the person as essentially the person he is. For what he thinks very worthwhile doing, and what he thinks very important not to do, contributes essentially to his being one sort of person rather than another. Whether or not a moral agent preserves his identity depends on whether or not he possesses integrity.

1

The person of integrity is sometimes seen as the person who possesses certain moral virtues. Most obviously, she will be honest in various ways: she does not systematically deceive, she does not cheat or break her word. She will, it seems, possess those virtues which may be labelled 'forms of conscientiousness', viz., honesty, fairness, truthfulness, and being a person of one's word.[2] But there is also what seems to be quite a different aspect of integrity, and one more closely linked to the etymology of the term (*integritas*: wholeness): the person of integrity is not corrupt, she is autonomous and takes responsibility for her choices and actions. What she does or chooses is truly hers.[3] If such considerations are centrally relevant to the question of whether or not a person possesses integrity then it is not enough to think of 'integrity' as simply a label for a set of virtues, and the question arises how these different, or seemingly different, aspects of integrity can be reconciled.

It is useful to start the discussion of integrity by considering again those individuals who are members of a group in virtue of their behaviour being governed by one honour-code. For

[1] This is only roughly true: changes in the identity of a person in so far as he is a moral agent may have repercussions; they may for example lead to the suppression or overemphasis of certain memories.

[2] The term is borrowed from James D. Wallace, *Virtues and Vices*, Contemporary Philosophy Series (Cornell University Press, 1978), Ch. IV.

[3] For this sort of view on integrity see Bernard Williams in 'A critique of utilitarianism' in Williams and Smart, *Utilitarianism For and Against* (CUP, 1973); and in 'Persons, Character and Morality' in *Moral Luck* (CUP, 1981); and also Peter Winch, 'Moral Integrity' in *Ethics and Action* (Routledge and Kegan Paul, 1972).

here we have a clear connection between a virtue or set of vir-tues which constitutes the person's 'honour', and that person's identity as dependent on his possessing the relevant virtues. Membership of the group entails living according to the values which are embodied in the code. Living accordingly, and only living accordingly, gives the individual status or worth, and his identity is defined in terms of that status. Any infringement of the code will undermine this status and undermine thereby his identity. The person's honour and his identity are therefore dependent on one another; they must stand or fall together.

It may seem that the notion of honour in the context of the shame-culture is a very restricted one with its socially imposed honour-code as the sole criterion of value, virtue, and identity. But of course the more complex the honour-code the richer the notion of honour that can be accommodated within this frame-work, and the greater the scope for the individual to fail to com-ply with the code because his interpretation of it is confused or superficial.[4] But however rich and complex the notion of honour in a particular culture may be, the reference to some accepted set of values remains prominent. Nowadays, when the notion of honour does not function conspicuously in our assess-ment of people, it is still most at home in those contexts where there are relatively clearly defined codes of behaviour. In a shame-culture, it could perhaps be said, the notions of honour and integrity coincide, whereas outside such a culture they may diverge. A soldier may lose his honour by some cowardly deed, but he may thereby not also lose his integrity, for he may not have had any integrity to lose. A person may become a candi-date for loss of honour simply by accepting a certain role which is governed by some specific code of behaviour. But such a move is not sufficient to make him a candidate for loss of integ-

---

[4] There are many illustrations of such difficulties in understanding or interpreting an honour-code in medieval literature. Chaucer's Criseyde, for instance, is confused: she is much concerned with her honour, but she takes this to refer primarily to her public reputation and neglects the requirements of loyalty. A case of too superficial an interpretation of the code is provided by Wolfram's Parzival: he fails to ask the right question about Amfortas' suffering because, lacking experience and maturity, he lets himself be guided by the words rather than the spirit of the knightly code. (*Parzival*, tr. H. M. Mustard and C. E. Passage (Vintage Books, N.Y., 1961), pp. 170–1.) See also *Sir Gawain and the Green Knight*, where Sir Gawain's interpretation of the code as applied to his own behaviour differs from that of King Arthur and the other knights: he sees cause for shame where they do not.

rity. Similarly, a soldier may lose honour according to the code but keep his integrity because the code does not seem to him to incorporate any important values at all. Unlike the member of the honour-group he dissociates himself from the values of his group. It is at least not a foregone conclusion that under such circumstances he must lose his integrity. In this sense honour remains tied to public codes and public opinion in a way in which integrity is not necessarily tied to these things.

If integrity is not necessarily linked to some public honour-code then it is much harder than it was in the case of honour to identify a person as a person of integrity, for there is now no obvious yardstick. Perhaps we try and cope with this difficulty by judging a person's possession or lack of integrity according to whether or not she possesses the virtues of conscientiousness. It is at least relatively easy to decide whether on some occasion a person has cheated, not kept her word, etc., and her behaviour over a range of such occasions may be thought to be sufficient to settle the question of her integrity. But if, like honour in the shame-culture, a person's integrity is also bound up with her identity then this cannot be explained by reference to these virtues, for the values embodied in them do not have the function in a society which the honour-code has in a shame-culture. If there is a comparable connection at all then it is not to be found if we look at the problem this way round. But it is still possible that the second suggestion of what we understand by integrity, that it has something to do with the 'wholeness' of the person, that the choices and actions of the person of integrity are peculiarly hers, will explain why it is right or at least natural to think of her as also possessing a certain set of virtues.

2

A person of integrity must at least be capable of evaluating different courses of action. This is a basic and minimal requirement, and one which has sometimes been put forward as being a condition which an individual has to fulfil to be a person at all.[5] I shall take Frankfurt's version of this proposal as the basis

[5] This is argued for by Harry Frankfurt, 'Freedom of the Will and the Concept of a Person', *Journal of Philosophy*, vol. lxviii, 1971. See also Daniel Dennett, 'Conditions of Personhood' in Oksenberg Rorty, ed., *The Identities of Persons* (University of California

for a discussion of the conditions which are necessary for possession of integrity. In his view one essential difference between
persons and other creatures is to be found in the person's will.
Their specific characteristic is that they are able to form what
he calls 'second-order volitions', which are desires directed
towards first-order desires. First-order desires are desires to do
or not to do one thing or another. But a first-order desire may
not play a significant role in what the person does or tries to do.
Whether it does or not depends on whether he wants that desire
to be effective or not. To have the capacity to form second-
order volitions is to have the capacity to want certain first-order
desires to be effective and to reject others. Thus, the person can
assess his desires, he is, as Frankfurt puts it, capable of reflective
self-evaluation. The desires he values, or wants to be effective,
he identifies with. He does not just intentionally act accordingly, but what he does he makes peculiarly his own by his will-
ing the desire in question to be effective. Desires he identifies
with cannot at the same time be disowned: a person cannot
identify with certain desires and yet regard them as something
that happens to him as if he were a helpless spectator. He is
involved with the desire and everything it prompts him to do.
To will some desires to be effective and others not is to be involved in the world as an agent with a certain amount of control
over what he does. At the same time, since this identification
requires at least a minimum degree of self-awareness and self-
assessment, he must also be capable of some self-detachment.

To be capable of valuing certain things and not valuing
others a person must be capable of having second-order volitions. Consequently, a person of integrity who (minimally)
must value certain things cannot be what Frankfurt calls a
'wanton'. A wanton is someone who lacks second-order volitions, and so is indifferent as to which of his first-order desires
is the strongest, and is also indifferent about which set of desires
to act on. A wanton does what he is most strongly inclined to
do and does not care what that is. But this cannot be true of the
person of integrity; he at the very least must identify with some
desires and not with others. It follows that, not being a wanton,

Press, 1976), pp. 175–94; and Charles Taylor, 'What is Human Agency?' in
Theodore Mischel, ed., *The Self* (Basil Blackwell, 1977), pp. 103–35.

the person of integrity does not act merely on those desires which happen to be strongest; he may decide to act on some desire which is weaker than a competing one. To this extent he is in control of his desires and not at their mercy. He will also engage in some form of reasoning: if he does not just act on whatever inclination happens to be the strongest he must have some reason for wanting one desire rather than another to be effective, though he need not necessarily be able to articulate that reason. From some point of view he thinks it more worthwhile to identify with a desire which is less strong than its competitors.

The person of integrity does not just act on a desire which happens to be strongest. 'Strongest desire' cannot here mean 'causally strongest desire', for the causally strongest desire is that which results in action. On this reading it is impossible that the agent, whether a person of integrity or not, should act on any but the strongest desire. For him to decide not to act on his strongest desire has to be understood as his deciding not to act on that desire which is phenomenologically the strongest. It presents itself to him as an inclination to act in a certain way which is stronger than any competitor. But the reasoning he engages in alters the causal efficacy of the competing desires.

The kind of valuing which consists in identification with some desires and rejection of others is all that Frankfurt's condition for personhood requires. He explicitly rejects any stronger sense of 'valuing' by allowing that:

a person may be capricious and irresponsible in forming his second-order volitions and give no serious consideration to what is at stake. Second-order volitions express evaluations only in the sense that they are preferences. There is no essential restriction on the kind of basis, if any, upon which they are formed. (p. 13 n. 6.)

The weak sense here given to what it is to value something may be all that is needed if the capacity to evaluate one's desires is to be a condition of personhood. But normally someone who formed his second-order volitions capriciously and irresponsibly would hardly be thought to be valuing anything at all. It is presumably open to him to identify with one set of desires today and with another tomorrow, depending perhaps on the convenience of circumstances or the company that happens to be present. On one occasion a person may identify with the desire to help another, but the identification may not survive that particular occasion. If this remains an isolated or merely capriciously repeated piece of behaviour then he cannot be said to value the well-being of another, or to value generous behaviour, and this will be so particularly if he does not even see a reason for helping another on other occasions as well. If he is to value such things then there must be some consistency in his identifications. The consistency is two-fold: a particular action resulting from his identification with some desire may have implications for his behaviour on future occasions, and these he cannot ignore. The most obvious case here is that of giving some undertaking. Secondly, the general description under which he sees what he is doing, whether this is, for example, 'helping others' or 'being a good friend to this particular neighbour', will also have implications for his behaviour on other occasions, and these he cannot ignore, either, if he is to value the desire as described. For an agent to value something there must be relevant behaviour patterns which fit the description of what it is he values.

The person who capriciously and irresponsibly identifies with different desires behaves as if what he says and does were isolated events with no implications for the future, and equally with no roots in the past. He does not grasp that choices have consequences, and so distances himself from them. While at one time he identifies with some desire, or with a set of desires, at another he fails to identify with what is implied by his earlier identifications. His identifications are not consistent with one another and so lack all unity. As an evaluating agent he has no identity. He is the shallowly sincere:[6] he is sincere in that on any particular occasion he identifies with the desire which results in the relevant action. But his failure to take seriously the implications of such identification makes his security a very shallow one.

The shallowly sincere, in so far as he is shallowly sincere, is plainly not a candidate for the possession of integrity. On the contrary, however this possession may be understood, the shallowly sincere is one paradigm of what it is to lack integrity. He

---

[6] The term is Fingarette's: *Self-Deception* (Routledge and Kegan Paul, 1977), pp. 51–2.

is incapable of valuing anything except in the very weak sense of evaluation offered by Frankfurt. But a stronger sense is needed if it is possession of integrity that is in question, and this requires constraints on the manner of the person's identification with his desires: he must be reasonably consistent in his identification with at any rate some desires or sets of desires.

In the weak sense of evaluating the person concerned need give no serious consideration to what is at stake and there is no restriction on the kind of basis on which his second-order volitions are formed. But some constraints are needed here, too, and for the same reason: if an agent gave no consideration to his identifications with first-order desires then we should not accept that he *valued* the type of behaviour in question.

The first constraint needed here arises from a consideration already mentioned. The introduction of the capacity to form second-order volitions rules it out that the agent always simply acts on those desires which at the time happen to be strongest. So he will sometimes at least have some reason for identifying with a desire for which his reason is not merely 'I just very much want this'. Some other consideration must affect the agent's identification, if only the thought that acting on this (weaker) desire will contribute more to his overall and long-term desire-satisfaction than would acting on the competing (stronger) desire. If this condition is not at least sometimes fulfilled then again the individual could hardly be said to value anything at all.

For a person to value something he must think it important to have or do that thing. There are degrees of valuing, but to whatever extent he values it he cannot abandon what he values merely for a whim. He cannot change his identifications lightly, he must have a reason for this change where the reason is thought by him to provide justification for what he is doing. It is doubtful that an appeal to overall desire-satisfaction will always count as justificatory, but in so far as this sort of consideration will force the agent to be selective about his desires and to recognize that it would be folly to act on some and good to act on others, it will do for present purposes as a case of the sort of reasoning required. However, if 'this course of action will yield maximum desire-satisfaction' is to be acceptable as a justificatory reason then the agent cannot believe it to be a reason just for him. If he justifies his change of evaluations on these grounds then he must allow others to do the same, for he would be inconsistent in claiming that what justifies his behaviour will not justify that of another in similar circumstances.

An agent who identifies with some first-order desire makes the choice of behaviour her own. She has exercised some control, and this is what we expect of someone whom we regard as an agent. It is also the case that a person who values something thinks that thing (relatively) important, and this thought is given substance by the agent's identification. But this is not always enough for the person to make what she is said to value her own, and for her exercising control over her desires. For her second-order volition may not be her own. This would be so were she to accept certain values just because they were the values of some group, and she is quite prepared without further thought to change her values should the group change theirs or should she happen to change groups. Her only reason for a change in evaluations is that she is now told differently what is good and what is not by those who, she thinks, will know. Under these circumstances she has hardly made the group's values her own: she has to find out from others which desires to identify with, or indeed what sorts of desires she should have. In such a case she seems to have abdicated control over her identifications and values. Even should she have a general desire always to be guided by the group she is with this would still leave her without control over any particular choice. Such a person would closely resemble the shallowly sincere, for her identifications being so ill-founded it is wholly accidental if she fulfils the conditions of consistency outlined earlier. In this case it is not a capricious change of mind on her part which may prevent her from doing so, but it is a change in circumstance which is capricious also, in the sense that it is unrelated to her previous identifications. To rule out such abdication of control there must be constraints not just on the manner of the identifications but also on their nature: if an agent is to value something and to have control over her values then (at least) her wanting some desire to be effective must be based on some reason such that any reason she accepts in favour of a change in identification must be thought to override it. For this to be possible it, the earlier reason, must have a role to play in that person's practical reasoning.

On the present account an agent can be said to value something only if his relevant identifications are reasonably consistent and if he engages in some form of practical reasoning, however rudimentary. This will be the sense in which valuing is to be understood in the rest of the chapter. Although 'valuing' now clearly has a stronger sense than that proposed by Frankfurt, it does not yet reflect all that valuing involves. To value something is to regard that thing as of value, where this value does not consist in just being the satisfaction of some desire of the agent in question. She must see that in virtue of which she values it as being other than and independent of its capacity to satisfy some desire of hers. She cannot, therefore, think of it as being a good just for herself, and the reasons which in her view justify her to act in this rather than any other way will not refer to just her own maximum desire-satisfaction. She cannot explain the point of what she wants and does by referring merely to what *she* likes or dislikes, what *she* finds fun to do or finds unpleasant. The point of her thinking one course of action more worthwhile than another must be that it is directed towards something which it is at least possible to conceive of as a (human) good. This is evidently a stronger requirement than the universalizability one mentioned earlier, which ruled merely that if an agent thinks she is justified in acting on such desires in some situation then she must accept that others, too, would be justified in acting on such desires in relevantly similar situations. There was no reference to what the agent thought objectively, i.e., independently of her desires, to be of value. Unlike the requirement of universalizability, the present requirement is explanatory of and gives point to her decision to act in one way rather than another. The overall support for this strong sense of valuing rests on the shortcomings of a non-cognitive theory of value.[7] In the account of integrity that follows I have not, however, essentially relied on this strong sense of evaluation.

---

[7] For a discussion of this theory see David Wiggins, 'Truth, Invention and the Meaning of Life', *Proceedings of the British Academy*, Vol. lxii (1976).

3

The person of integrity must be capable of evaluating and thereby controlling her desires in a sense which is stronger than that given by Frankfurt. In this sense not every exercise of a second-order volition constitutes an evaluation; it is an evaluation only if certain other conditions are also fulfilled. Where the desires a person wants to be effective are such evaluations there will be some degree of coherence among them. This is so partly because fulfilling the condition of consistency provides for patterns of behaviour over some areas, and partly because fulfilling the condition of engaging in some practical reasoning prohibits a change of identification which is quite unconnected with all previous identifications. With both these conditions fulfilled evaluating cannot be a wholly superficial and short-lived affair, and a change in identifications cannot be an isolated occurrence but will have more or less far-reaching repercussions, depending on the type of evaluation in question. Changing one's evaluations, therefore, is something of an upheaval in a person's life, and for this reason, too, is not something that is undertaken lightly.

Evaluations result in actions. This is so by definition, for they have been presented as a sub-class of second-order volitions, and nothing counts as a second-order volition unless it results in action or attempted action. This is acceptable from one point of view: what an agent values should be expressed in her actions unless on that occasion it conflicts with the expression of a desire she values more. This is the paradigm case. The less her evaluations are expressed in action the more suspect the claim that she values the relevant type of behaviour.[8] It would, however, be too extreme a step to make it true by definition that evaluations are expressed in action and so to rule out without further consideration that she may value certain

[8] This of course depends on how highly she values the type of behaviour in question; if she values it just a little it may never be expressed in action because always overridden by something she values more. There are also cases where a person may think of certain sorts of behaviour as expressing values which ought to be in the world, but she does not attempt to act accordingly because she believes that she, e.g., lacks the necessary strength or skill, or because engaging in that enterprise would interfere too much with other activities she wants to be involved in more. The assumption in the chapter is that what the agent values or disvalues is more centrally related to how she conducts her life.

desires although she does not often act on them. It would also be inconvenient to do so. For linking evaluations with actions by definition makes it impossible to speak of evaluations as entering into the agent's deliberations. But in shifting from a weak to a stronger sense of evaluating the agent's reasoning prior to action has acquired more significance, and so it is important to be able to speak of the role of evaluations in deliberation where it cannot be true of them that they are expressed in action. From the deliberator's point of view a person will see the desires she values as those she has reason to identify with consistently. Evaluations as now understood must present themselves to the deliberating agent as overriding any competing weak evaluations. It follows from their respective characterization that she must see reason to engage on the course of action prescribed by strong evaluations, a reason which does not apply to weak evaluations. From some point of view she believes that course of action to be worthwhile even if it should conflict with other and possibly stronger desires. Should she act against her evaluations she will have acted against what in her own view is the better reason.

The person of integrity will not repeatedly act against her evaluations. The desires she values above others she will identify with and act upon. She will thereby acknowledge them publicly and so take responsibility for what she values. This much I take to be plainly true of such a person. But this characterization has wider implications. In evaluating possible courses of action she will see some of her desires as from some point of view not worthwhile and so not identify with them and not act upon them, either because she does not think that such desires should ever be acted upon, or because on this occasion they clash with an evaluation. She will nevertheless acknowledge such desires in the sense of recognizing them for what they are, for failure to do so may be a threat to her being clear about her evaluations. She may also desire to have desires she does not in fact have, and given she thinks such desires worthwhile she will make some attempt to acquire them. In acknowledging the relative merit of her desires she will give appropriate weight to her reasons for action.

This greatly oversimplified and idealized picture of flawless practical reasoning ascribes to the person of integrity considerable clarity of vision. She knows what her desires are worth and acts accordingly. To speak of her as 'acknowledging' her desires seems to imply that desires are given and are what they are, and that in acknowledging them we simply recognize them for what they are. But sometimes what we desire may be a matter not of discovery but of decision, for we shape and do not just discover what we are. Speaking of decision here is, however, also misleading: we do not freely choose what we are, either; we cannot just turn ourselves into anything we like. So neither alternative will quite do. 'Acknowledging desires' should not be taken to imply that desires, in being acknowledged, are named or described as objects whose existence is quite independent of the name-giver and hence quite unaffected by the name or description. Naming desires requires not only some interpretation of what there is, but also affects and changes what there is. In a paper on human agency Charles Taylor speaks in this context of the 'articulation' of desires.[9] In articulating our likes and dislikes, what we think worthwhile, unimportant or unworthy, we do not precisely choose our desires. But nor are we left entirely at their mercy, for our articulations give them shape. They attempt to formulate and thereby to impose some order on what is chaotic or confused. Articulations make desires what they are; they are therefore at least partially constitutive of the desires in question.

If a person of integrity has to publicly acknowledge her evaluations, in the sense of acting on them, and also has to acknowledge in the sense of articulating desires not to be acted on, or to be acted on only if they do not clash with evaluations, then possession of integrity demands a degree of self-knowledge and self-control which it is no doubt impossible for anyone to achieve. Even less would it be possible for anyone, whether the agent or some observer, to know that it has been achieved. Integrity remains an ideal, though under certain circumstances we may deem that someone fulfils all the conditions. But a list of major flaws in practical reasoning should at least give us some sufficient conditions for lack of integrity, and give us necessary conditions, therefore, for its possession.

The person whose practical reasoning does not go astray will act on those desires she most values, she will not act against her

9 Ed. Mischel *The Self*, particularly pp. 13–14.

better judgement. But she may be confused or ambiguous about what her better judgement actually amounts to. In particular, she may only think or like to think that she values certain desires when in fact she does not; there may be an element of self-deception in her evaluations. Where a person is self-deceived there are contradictions and ambiguities in her identifications. In Sartre's well-known case of self-deception a young woman is so engrossed in her intellectual talk about Life that she does not 'notice' her hand being left in that of the man's.[10] What she values, she thinks, are the important things which make life worth living: her freedom, intellect, and consciousness. She tries to reconcile this view of herself, as caring for the intellectual and spiritual only, with the sexual implications of leaving her hand where it is, by disowning the hand; it is no part of her and she need pay no attention to it. Her (unacknowledged) desire to leave her hand where it is is incompatible with her view of herself. She does and does not identify with that desire. If she did not identify with it at all, she would withdraw her hand; if she fully identified with it she would acknowledge to herself what she is doing. Wishing to maintain her flattering view of herself she cannot afford to articulate that desire.

Such distortions of evaluations can be seen particularly clearly in the case of someone whose whole life is based on a piece of self-deception. A character from George Eliot's *Middlemarch* supplies such a case: Mr. Casaubon values creative scholarship above all, and the only worthwhile life for him to lead is the life of the creative scholar. So he devotes himself to the writing of a scholarly masterpiece, and everything else in his life, such as the work in his parish and his marriage to Dorothea, is subordinated to this task. But he has reason to fear that this masterpiece is not really flourishing and that his scholar's life is not what it ought to be. In order for this fear not to emerge into the open and to be seen as justified he has to take steps to protect himself: he isolates himself from other scholars, refuses to learn German, discourages his wife's searching questions, and so on. This kind of behaviour is not the behaviour of a creative scholar. The more such steps he is forced to take the more his life diverges from the kind of life he thought it worthwhile to lead, and the more he tries to maintain

---

[10] *Being and Nothingness* (Methuen, 1981), pp. 55–6.

his identification with Casaubon the scholar the less does he in fact so identify. His life is no longer governed by what he believes he values most, for what he now identifies with is no longer, or is only partially, the type of behaviour which expresses scholarly values, but is his desire to cling to the favoured picture of himself and thus to avoid the shattering experience of having to reassess himself and the life he leads. Hence there are incompatible strands in his life: it is now governed by certain unacknowledged desires, but there is no point in it being so governed without the initial evaluations. There would be no need for his persisting in living as he does if he could envisage another form of life as being as or more worthwhile for him to lead. So at one and the same time he has both to confirm and deny his evaluations, and so also confirm and deny his identity in terms of these evaluations. He identifies with the wishful thought that he is leading a scholar's life, but much of his behaviour denies this identification. His scholar's identity is thereby frustrated and corrupted, and as he refuses to reassess the situation no other identity has a chance to flourish.

In a case of this sort of self-deception the practical reasoning touching on the relevant areas of the person's life is flawed, as the reasons on which his conclusions are based and which appear to him justificatory are not in fact the reasons on which he acts, while on the other hand the desires which play a central role in his behaviour he could not conceivably regard as justificatory. In not articulating these latter desires he cannot begin to try and control them, and this seriously interferes with his effectiveness as an agent. It may be that the exercise of control in this area is very limited, anyway. But unless desires are articulated they cannot be assessed at all, and so the person is not even in a position to consider whether or not he wants them to be effective.

The person who (seriously) deceives himself distorts his evaluations. To maintain such deception he cannot be open to any evidence that may interfere with it. In particular, he will have to make his conception of other people's reaction to him fit his image of himself, and so distort or ignore what is unacceptable. As he presents himself to himself so he has to present himself to others, and he can take from others only what will support this presentation. In this way he can feed his self-deception. Although he may not succeed in deceiving others he will necessarily mis-present himself to them. To that extent the self-deceived is also hypocritical.

The seriously self-deceived does not possess integrity. This is not to say that in some respects his evaluations may not be perfectly straightforward. Mr. Casaubon is a man of conventional morality who would not dream, for example, of cheating his tradesmen or of not carrying out what he thinks it right to undertake, such as giving financial help to his cousin. In some respect and over some areas he may be said to act with integrity. But the distortion of his evaluations has various consequences which are incompatible with his possessing integrity: firstly, his control over his desires and thereby over the sort of life he wants to lead is seriously impaired. Secondly, he cannot face up to the truth and so must ignore the relevant evidence there is about himself. And finally, he is a deceiver of others, unconscious though that may be.

While on the one hand the self-deceived mis-presents himself to others, the hypocrite who fairly consistently presents himself to others as he is not is very likely to be also self-deceived. He does not have to ignore or distort the evidence about himself which there is in the reaction of others, but given that he is reasonably successful, the evidence will relate to the persona he presents to them, and not to the person whose evaluations are really quite different. So as evidence about himself the reaction of others is quite useless to him. In this state of isolation it is highly unlikely that someone who extensively and successfully misleads others can remain sufficiently detached and clear about what he is doing; it is far more likely that he too will slide into self-deception. But whether he does or not, it is true of, at any rate, the Tartuffe type hypocrite who just pretends to value or disvalue certain things that his evaluations must be distorted and his practical reasoning flawed. *Ex hypothesi*, he does not act on what he really values, so that he cannot will the relevant desires to be effective. On the other hand, his behaviour is not prompted by the sorts of desires which normally motivate that type of behaviour. So there is here a break between motive and action which is contrary to proper evaluation. Unlike the self-deceived he may have articulated his desires; he does not, however, acknowledge publicly what it is he values and so does not take responsibility for it.

This type of hypocrite is plainly not a person of integrity, and in general to present oneself to others as one knows or suspects one is not, to mislead as to what one's thoughts and judgements actually are, is a prima-facie case of loss or lack of integrity. But there are exceptions. Beethoven's Leonora, for example, is quite acceptably presented as a person of integrity, and that even though her behaviour towards the prison warder and his family is that of a hypocrite. In her case, it seems, deceiving others does not undermine her integrity. The first important feature of the case is that she greatly regrets the need for her deception. The fact that such-and-such behaviour constitutes a piece of deception must always, for the person of integrity, be a reason against behaving in this way. Nor can it be a reason which in her view is easily overridden, for to deceive lightly over a range of occasions leads to the distortions in evaluations and reasoning already discussed. It is also true of Leonora that she is quite clear why she has to engage in deceptive behaviour, she is quite clear that it is an unavoidable evil if she is to act on those desires with which she most essentially identifies. She is above all the loyal wife who has to bring about her husband's release from prison, and not to pursue the relevant course of action would be far more undermining of her integrity than her temporary piece of deception can be. She has, and is quite clear that she has, sufficient reason for action.

4

On the view here discussed, lack of control over what a person does is the crucial factor responsible for lack or loss of integrity. In order to remain in control it is necessary for the agent to be clear about her evaluations, and this in turn implies that there cannot be unacknowledged desires which seriously interfere with these evaluations. She has to be honest with herself. She will also be honest with others in that she will express in her actions what she values most and thereby take responsibility for it. Failure to do so is always a threat to her evaluations, at least if it is at all frequent or prolonged. It will tend to weaken and confuse them. If failing to act according to her evaluations is not to be a case of loss of integrity she must at least be quite clear why she acts as she does. From this point of view the not fully conscious deception of others perpetrated by the self-deceived is worse than the calculated deception of the hypocrite, just because the self-deceived does not know that she is doing.

Bruno Bettelheim, in an essay about life in a concentration camp, seems to have in mind the notion of integrity as it is here outlined. He writes:

To survive as a man, not a walking corpse, as a debased and degraded but still human being, one had first and foremost to remain informed and aware of what made up one's personal point of no return beyond which one would never, under any circumstances, give in to the oppressor, even if it meant risking and losing one's life. It meant being aware that if one survived at the price of overreaching this point one would be holding on to a life that had lost all meaning. It would mean surviving—not with lower self-respect, but without any . . .

Second in importance was keeping oneself informed of how one felt about complying when the ultimate decision as to where to stand firm was not called in question . . . One had to comply with debasing and amoral commands if one wished to survive; but one had to remain cognizant that one's reason for complying was 'to remain alive and unchanged as a person'. Therefore, one had to decide, for any given action, whether it was truly necessary for one's safety or that of others, and whether committing it was good, neutral or bad. This keeping informed and aware of one's actions—though it could not alter the required act—this minimal distance from one's own behaviour, and the freedom to feel differently about it depending on its character, this too was what permitted the prisoner to remain a human being. (From *Surviving and Other Essays*, Thames & Huelsou 1979)

In contrast to those who are not at all clear about their personal point of no return, the prisoner who, while forced to do what he thinks degrading, knows what he is doing and why, saves his integrity. He is not corrupted by the treatment he receives or by the sort of behaviour forced upon him. Even though he has no control over what he actually does, he at least retains control over his evaluations in the sense of being sure which sorts of desires he would consistently want to be effective in any circumstances other than these extreme ones. He is very different from someone who has lost the degree of control he still possesses and just acts from that desire which at the time is the

strongest.[11] To maintain that much control under such circumstances is of course a considerable achievement, and there must
always be the threat of its being undermined. Public acknowledgement of one's evaluations is the only safeguard against
such threats. But while such acknowledgement is therefore very
important for integrity, the lack of it on some occasions is not
by itself sufficient for integrity to be lost.

An account of integrity as being primarily a matter of the
agent's control over what she is doing explains the type of
behaviour we expect of a person we regard as having integrity.
To be a candidate for possession of integrity the person's
choices and evaluations must be her own: her identifications
with her desires must be neither subject to unconsidered
change nor be distorted or confused. Her reasons for action
must be genuine. Such integrity cannot be maintained without
a degree of courage: she cannot fail to do or say what she thinks
she should even on those occasions when she finds it difficult to
do so. This is so because, by and large, her actions must accord
with her evaluations. She will stand by her values and not be
bribed to act against them, whether the source of the bribe is in
herself or in others. In publicly acknowledging her evaluations
she accepts responsibility for what she does. For to explain
away her actions, or find excuses for them, is to disown what
she sets store by. It is then not surprising that honesty and up-
rightness should be seen as the mark of the person of integrity.

But this is not to say that the exercise of such virtues is
enough to justify our verdict. For acting with integrity on some
occasion it is sufficient that a person should act as her values
dictate. But a person may so act on numerous occasions (as,
e.g., Mr. Casaubon does) and yet it would not be true that he
possesses integrity; for acting with integrity over a range of
occasions is compatible with muddled evaluations and serious
self-deception. In so far as ascription of possession of integrity
is based on a person acting with integrity, the ascription goes
beyond the support there is for it. But in other respects ascriptions are sometimes too narrowly based: we are perhaps inclined

---

[11] Contrast the case of Bettelheim's prisoner with that of Winston in Orwell's *1984*.
The latter loses his integrity when, under threat of unbearable torture, he betrays his
love for Julia. He loses his ability to discriminate and so loses all control over his
action.

to pick out the more spectacular occasions, those which involve a public stand against authority or popular opinion. But acting with integrity does not necessarily involve making such a stand, there need be nothing spectacular about it. Again, we may be inclined to pick out those occasions for ascription of integrity when the value the person stands up for is one we think admirable. But the nature of what the person concerned thinks so important is also not relevant to whether or not he has acted with integrity. It could be said of Don Giovanni that he acts with integrity at that moment when the imminent prospect of the fires of hell does not make him disown his way of life. But there is nothing to admire in the Don's way of life.

Just as our ascriptions of integrity tend to be based on the exercise of moral excellences and therefore function as expressions of praise, so are our ascriptions of lack or loss of integrity correspondingly based on the exercise of the relevant moral failings, and function as expressions of blame. There is here again a discrepancy between the ascription of and the actual lack of integrity, though of a different kind. The lack of certain moral qualities, such as honesty and courage, is indeed sufficient for lack of integrity, but there are also cases of lack of integrity where we do not make the corresponding judgement, for they are not the consequence of moral shortcomings and so not a matter for blame. The severely mentally ill will lack integrity, at least during the period of their illness.[12] Ascriptions of lack or loss of integrity try to draw a line between those who are responsible for their actions and those who are not, but such a distinction is not always relevant to the lack of integrity itself. Naturally enough, what we take the trouble to identify and comment on will fall into an area in which we not only have a particular interest, but where we also believe ourselves to be competent to judge, and so we tend to rely on moral shortcomings in our ascriptions of lack or loss of integrity.

If it is a person's evaluations and her ordering of these evaluations which are crucial to integrity then there is of course no

---

[12] e.g. the schizophrenic, whose 'real' or 'inner' self is totally withdrawn and is isolated from the self as expressed in his actions, lacks integrity. But this is not to say that any period of mental illness or every mental breakdown is destructive of the person's integrity. The loss of control may not be serious or long enough to have that effect. Or it may be that the agent can come to terms with such periods of illness and not let them interfere too much with the kind of life he thinks he should live.

guarantee that these are widely shared and acceptable, or that the values in question are particularly moral. The person of integrity need not be a morally good person, she may not be much, or possibly not be at all, moved by other-regarding reasons. But at least she cannot wholly ignore others. This point is connected with the requirement that she must be clear about her evaluations. She must get her practical reasoning right and act on that reason which, all things considered, she thinks best. But to have any thought about what might or might not be important to pursue in her life she cannot treat herself as if she were an isolated being. If she is to have a sane view of herself and the life she wants to lead she cannot ignore the evidence of her impact on others and their reactions to her. She must therefore give some recognition to others as persons who have views and interests and intentions of their own. Nor can she see others simply as providers of evidence about herself. For it is not possible that her impact on others could be understood by her were she to abstract their reactions to her from the context of general social communication. The evidence about herself which she could gather under such circumstances would be bound to be distorted. Her recognition of others cannot, therefore, be a wholly superficial one. She cannot be indiscriminate about the evidence that comes her way, either, for not everything will be equally worth having. So she will have to assess the views of others, and their evaluations. But this again cannot leave altogether untouched her own evaluations. It may be that these are now shown up as being shallow or short-sighted. The suppression of or turning away from such evidence about herself and her values would be a threat to her integrity. Unless she is open to such evidence her pattern of reasoning is likely to remain unexamined and static, and is unlikely to reflect as it should the wider and more varied experiences of a person capable of change and development.

If it is true that the person of integrity must be aware of others to the extent described then there is perhaps a closer link between integrity and morality than was earlier suggested. At least the person of integrity cannot be a moral solipsist, for she will recognize that others, too, are evaluators who, in so far as they act with integrity, act on reasons which they regard as justificatory. It is a reasonable assumption (and one to which

I shall return) that her self-respect is not independent of her integrity: she respects herself in so far as she acts with integrity. If so, then it would seem unreasonable and even inconsistent of her to withhold respect from others who also act according to their evaluations. But to respect others, if it is not to remain an empty phrase, must mean that to some extent at least consideration of their rights and interests will figure in that person's practical reasoning.[13]

Integrity as here understood has as its opposite corruption in quite a literal sense. In that sense corruption is a destruction or dissolution of the constitution which makes a thing what it is. That which is corrupt falls apart and cannot flourish. A person is in this sense corrupt if her identifications with various desires conflict and therefore thwart one another. In the cases of the shallowly sincere and of the seriously and centrally self-deceived the contradictions are such that no self has a chance to flourish. There is no proper identity in that there are no relatively consistent identifications. Any possible identity is thwarted by competing identifications. Lack of integrity does not mean lack of overall unity, of sets of identifications which all cohere with each other. It means the mutual undermining of identifications. This is also true of various brands of hypocrites. They do not just separate their inner from their outer lives, or their deeds from their words, but what they do or say contradicts what they really want to identify with. If the identity of the moral agent is given by her identifications then lack of integrity will, by interfering with such identifications, also destroy the identity of that agent.

A corrupted identity, then, is one where there are a number of identifications which are mutually stultifying; where this state obtains there is lack of integrity. Any particular loss of integrity on some particular occasion is corruptive in that it may bring about that state of affairs. The factors I have picked out as being responsible for such corruption are deceit, especially towards oneself, and lack of control. It may now seem

---

[13] It may be possible to establish other links between integrity and morality: e.g. Mary Midgley argues that a lasting divorce between the inner and outer life is a denial of reason and sanity. In 'The Objection to Systematic Humbug', *Philosophy* liii (1978). See also Bernard Mayo's paper 'Moral Integrity', where he wants to show that 'personal' integrity is much the same thing as 'moral' integrity: *Human Values*, Royal Institute of Philosophy Lectures, Vol. xi (1976–7).

that the person of integrity has to be self-analytical, highly articulate, and quite lacking in spontaneity. For to be in control he was required to articulate his desires and to go through a process of (flawless) practical reasoning. But it would clearly be a mistake to insist on these properties and thereby to rule out the inarticulate and not particularly self-aware as candidates for the possession of integrity. Nor are such properties required. To articulate one's desires is not necessarily to put into words what these desires are. They are articulated also by being expressed in non-verbal behaviour, provided the agent does not turn a blind eye towards what he is doing, as did the young woman in Sartre's case of self-deception. But the kind of awareness needed does not demand that the person concerned be highly articulate. Charles Taylor, from whom the notion of articulating one's desires was taken, speaks of giving our motivation a formulation in terms of words or *images* ('What is Human Agency?' p. 126, my italics). This suggests that the 'articulation' may also consist in the person envisaging certain situations, or certain responses to a given situation, and then accepting or rejecting the picture so evoked: it may or may not 'feel right'. It is similarly the case that practical reasoning need not be highly articulate, nor need the agent go consciously through the steps. Conscious practical reasoning is often quite unnecessary, for over a whole range of behaviour people are likely to take their evaluations for granted and so to act on them as a matter of course. They become conscious of such evaluations only when the relevant values are threatened. There is nothing wrong with that, provided it does not lead to an inflexibility in evaluations when the person concerned has reason to change them.

5

A moral agent's evaluation will range from the (in her view) centrally important to the quite trivial. Given sound practical reasoning, more or less trivial evaluations will be expressed in action only if they do not conflict with more important ones; whether this happens rarely or frequently will depend on the circumstances of the agent's life. Being on the periphery of her sets of values any change in them will not have particularly far-reaching consequences on the nature and order of her other evaluations. They therefore do not contribute to her identity and have nothing to do with her possession or lack of integrity. Only those evaluations have bearing on this question which figure prominently as overriding reasons in the agent's practical reasoning. I shall refer to these as the agent's 'commitments'.

Of the emotions of self-assessment discussed, shame and guilt are essentially connected with a person's integrity, though the details of the connection are different in the two cases. In the case of shame the connection is through self-respect. A person can have self-respect, or a sense of her own value, only if she believes some form of life is worth living, and believes that by and large she is capable of leading such a life. Self-respect must be based on what she takes to be her commitments, for it must be based on that in virtue of which she thinks herself worthy of respect, and she cannot think herself worthy of respect in virtue of something which she herself regards as relatively trivial. That is, to have self-respect she must have a degree of integrity; without some integrity there would be no self to respect.[14] And further, if integrity is the identity of the person in terms of her commitments then self-respect protects this identity by protecting the relevant values: the person who has self-respect will not tolerate certain types of behaviour on her own part, nor certain types of treatment offered her by others. As a person's commitments are normally varied and cover different areas of activity, it is possible to maintain self-respect with regard to some areas and not with regard to others. She may believe that some of her evaluations have implications which she feebly ignores, or that some areas of her life are not governed by the sorts of values by which they ought to be governed.

Shame is felt about injury to, or loss, or lack of self-respect. At the moment of experiencing shame the person believes that some of her important expectations concerning what is due to or from her have been frustrated. She thinks, possibly only

[14] She must *have* some integrity, rather than merely *think* she has. If she only thinks she more or less consistently acts according to her evaluations when in fact she does not she would obviously be self-deceived to a considerable extent. But the point of such self-deception would be to persuade herself that she can (still) respect herself, an exercise which would be unnecessary if she had self-respect anyway.

briefly, that her commitments are not the right ones, or that she does not live up to them, or that she lacks commitments altogether in an area where she ought to have them. If, broadly, every case of feeling shame is a case of perceived injury to self-respect, and if self-respect is connected with integrity in the way just described, then there should be some connection also between shame and integrity. This connection is not hard to see: those occasions where the perceived injury to my self-respect is due to my thinking my evaluations shoddy or my actions contrary to their dictates are also occasions of my perceiving a threat to my integrity—whether or not I myself describe my awareness in these terms. That is to say, whenever I feel shame about something I have done or have omitted to do then I will see a threat to my integrity; for shame is about my shortcomings with respect to formulating or living up to my commitments. But not all cases of shame are of this sort. I may feel shame not about something I have done, but feel it rather about the deed or state of somebody else to whom I see myself as so related that his defects reflect on my worth. My father has done something disgraceful, and the sense of my value based on the conception of being the daughter of this father is now undermined. But this does not seem to constitute a threat to my integrity. Whether or not there is such a threat depends rather on how I cope with the new situation. I may (or may not) react in a way which amounts to a betrayal of what I value, and then of course loss of integrity is involved. But the feeling of shame occasioned by my father's doings is as such unrelated to my integrity as there is here no conflict of identifications. Such cases of shame seem to fall outside the area of integrity, except that they put the person concerned in a position where her reactions have some bearing on her integrity.

But there is another point to be made about such a case: it may be that what I value most in life is being a good daughter to my father, and my father now behaves in such a way that I cannot have the kind of relationship to him which a good daughter can be expected to have. There does seem to be a threat to my integrity here, for the desires I most want to be effective now cannot be effective. If they are such central desires as the story assumes then my integrity must be involved. But this is a rather different case from the earlier one: I am prevented from identifying in the way I should (given my values) and so my identifications are frustrated. This is different from acting against my evaluations, as I do when I am self-indulgent, cowardly, or hypocritical. It was in the sense of her identifications being frustrated that, in a shame-culture, a person involved in the disgrace brought about by another member of her family might be said to perceive a threat to her integrity. What in that setting is assumed, and makes the case plausible, is that the evaluations are given and that family disgrace has to be passively accepted as destructive of the member's status and identity.

To say that when feeling shame the agent's view of the situation can be described (over the range of cases indicated) as 'constituting a threat to her integrity' is not to say that her view is necessarily correct; what is perceived as a threat need not in fact be one. This is so where the person suffers from 'false' shame, the shame which is occasioned by the temporary acceptance of an alien standard, or by momentarily attaching a degree of importance to a piece of behaviour which the agent comes to see it does not deserve. Not living according to such a standard, or behaving in that way, does not in fact threaten the agent's integrity. But there is a threat here none the less, though not as perceived by her at the time, for she lets herself be muddled about her values. The threat may be quite minor, as it was in Faithful's case. But the more often a person suffers from false shame, the more serious the threat to her integrity, or the more indicative, perhaps, of confusion or uncertainty about her values.[15] It is the experiencing of shame itself which here constitutes the threat. There is a parallel between this case and that where a person does not feel shame although her integrity is threatened, for she is not aware of that fact. Here her lack of shame is an indication that the corruption is serious

[15] 'False shame' covers a range of cases. Faithful's shame is one type, Fanny Thornton's another:

'Mr. Thornton! Does he really find time to read with a tutor, in the midst of all his business,—and this abominable strike in hand as well?'

Fanny was not sure, from Mrs Slickson's manner, whether she ought to be proud or ashamed of her brother's conduct; and, like all people who try and take other people's 'ought' for the rule of their feelings, she was inclined to blush for any singularity of action. Her shame was interrupted by the dispersion of the guests.

(Elizabeth Gaskell, *North and South*, Ch. xx.)

indeed: not even to perceive an injury to self-respect must mean that the agent has lost grip on her evaluations. It was for this reason, I suggested earlier, that shame is regarded sometimes as a virtue.

While a perceived threat to integrity may or may not be an actual threat, it is always the case that a perceived injury to self-respect is in fact such an injury, even if what the person experiences is false shame. This is so because self-respect may be lost although there is nothing wrong with the person's evaluations. In rightly or wrongly believing something to be wrong she loses her confidence in her evaluations and so in her own worth. She is no longer sure that this is how she ought to behave or to be treated, and such lack of certainty affects her respect for herself. It is therefore possible that a person of integrity may have little or even no self-respect just because that person lacks confidence in her evaluations. But her integrity cannot under such circumstances be very secure, for her lack of confidence makes her the sort of person who is a likely prey to false shame. The relation of shame to integrity is therefore not always straightforward. It may be that what is perceived as constituting a threat to integrity is just that. In that case her shame is justified, in the sense that it relates to her genuine evaluations. (Whether or not it is objectively justified is of course a different question.) Where shame is in this sense unjustified the threat to integrity is still there, but it is not what in the agent's own view constitutes the threat. It is however still the injury to self-respect which makes integrity insecure, for lack of confidence in her commitments increases the chances of her practical reasoning being confused.

It is its relation to integrity which makes shame such a potentially devastating emotion. Guilt can be equally devastating. It, too, is related to integrity, though the perceived threat to integrity takes here a different form. In shame the self is seen as less worthy than the agent thought, assumed, or hoped he was or might become; such thoughts, hopes or assumptions have now turned out to be unfounded. When feeling guilt, on the other hand, the agent sees himself as the doer of a wicked deed and so as alien to himself; he sees another self emerging. The 'wicked deed' refers to his action (or omission) seen as violating some taboo, and the emerging self is the self capable of violating the taboo. In many ordinary cases of guilt, of course, the particular action or omission may not be thought by the agent to be a very serious violation, or not thought to be the violation of a very serious taboo. In such a case the second self does not have much substance; its appearance is only fleeting and so is not much of a threat. As in shame there is here a range of cases vastly differing in degrees of severity. But if in feeling guilt the agent thinks of himself as having done something he regards as alien to himself and which yet has been brought about by him, then there is here the danger of a split, however fleeting that danger might be. Once there is this danger then there is also the possibility that the alien self, the doer of the forbidden deed, might assume control, and so what is important to the person feeling guilt is to purge himself of that self and thereby to regain his (degree of) integrity. Guilt, then, is different from shame in that it is not felt at the recognition of the failure of the worthy self, but is felt rather at the recognition of the emergence of a worse self. It is therefore also differently related to integrity. The person feeling guilt does not perceive an injury to his self-respect, it is not his worth which is primarily his concern. The self he is aware of is alien precisely because its deed expresses an evaluation which is not his own. Such a self is unrelated to his self-respect, or becomes a candidate for self-respect only if, like Macbeth, he tries to realign himself. It is because the alien evaluation interferes with his own that the person feeling guilt sees a threat to his integrity.

These differences between the two emotions explain other contrasting features. They explain why guilt but not shame is rightly connected with fear and anxiety:[16] an alien self whose doings conflict with the agent's evaluations is indeed something to fear and feel anxious about. In shame the agent sees himself diminished, and a diminished self need not be feared; it is just something to be despised. The emerging alien self, on the other hand, is not despicable, it has after all not been a failure but has on the contrary made its mark. So a person feeling guilty may not be without a feeling of pride in what he has done. Although what he did was wrong, in breaking a command (it may seem to him) he has at least done something positive, and

[16] e.g. Freud, *Civilization and its Discontents*, Section VII.

in this he may conceivably see cause for self-admiration. Of course feelings of pride would be quite incompatible with feeling shame. A person cannot despise and admire himself at the same time. He has, in his view, failed to have the right values, or failed to be clear about them, or failed to act in such a manner that his behaviour unambiguously expresses his values. Shame is always felt about some failure of this kind, and so the self always appears weak and ineffectual. For this reason there is in cases of shame a loss of confidence in either his values or in his capacity to live up to them which is not to be found in cases of guilt.

There are consequently types of behaviour which seem more appropriate occasions for shame than for guilt, and the other way about. The response to an obviously aggressive and violent deed, such as murder, would perhaps more naturally be expected to be guilt rather than shame, and that to what are plainly failures, such as avoidance of discomfort, ridicule, or danger, to be shame and not guilt. But of course it all depends on how the agent himself sees the situation. The killer may be struck not by the violence of his action but by its failure to comply with his code of conduct, and the coward may be impressed not by his failure but by his acting against his obligations as he sees them.

The same type of behaviour, such as telling a lie, may be an occasion for guilt, or for shame, or both. If it is an occasion for guilt the agent will see telling the lie as something he must not do. Telling the truth is obligatory and remains obligatory however good the reasons may be for on this occasion acting otherwise. If it is an occasion for shame then it is out of respect for himself that he tells the truth. He owes it to himself to do so, it is beneath him, he is too proud to tell a lie. In each case the motivation differs from the motives that prompt either prudential or other-regarding actions. In that case the agent's reasons for action can be stated in terms of the aim he has in mind in acting as he does: he tells the truth to serve his own best interests or those of another. This is not so in the former case: the agent does not act in order to do what is obligatory, or in order to preserve his self-respect. At most the reference to obligation and self-respect indicates that there are such reasons, which would be reasons for his evaluations being what they are. In particular, a person acting out of self-respect does not act in order to preserve his integrity, or to keep himself morally pure. As Bernard Williams has pointed out, such desires can hardly be a person's primary motive for action, for to have such a desire the agent first needs something to be pure about.[17] If, then, the charge that acting with integrity may be acting self-indulgently is based on the thought that self-respect (or for that matter, integrity) generates the kind of reason the description of which completes an 'in order to . . . ' formulation, then this charge is indeed misplaced. The mistake would not just be in turning 'acting out of self-respect' into the sort of reason which it is not; it would lie also in trying to find at all an isolated reason for the action which will explain just it. A person acts out of self-respect when he does what he feels himself committed to, and the reasons for the action are those which have played a part in determining his commitments. But commitments are deeply rooted and have implications which are likely to be far-reaching. To pick out just one reason as giving the aim of this particular action would hardly be adequate as either an explanation or justification of what he is doing.

Acting out of self-respect, while it is not acting in order to protect the person's integrity, nevertheless does protect it, and so is a bonus for the agent. Whether or not this particular action is generally beneficial is quite a different question and depends partly on the nature of the agent's evaluations. In acting out of self-respect his thoughts are on his commitments rather than on himself, the focus is primarily on the action and not on the actor. But of course they are *his* commitments, they embody the values he thinks make his life worthwhile. So the self is obliquely involved. By contrast, self-esteem is more directly centred on the self.

The two emotions concerned with self-esteem are pride and humiliation. In contrast to guilt and shame, emotional pride is not essentially connected with integrity. This is not to say that a person may not be proud of having acted with integrity, or of being a person of integrity. He may well see reason for self-esteem in the fact that his commitments are of a certain kind and that he acts accordingly on relevant occasions. But pride

[17] Bernard Williams, 'Utilitarianism and moral self-indulgence', in *Moral Luck*, pp. 48–9.

need not take this direction. The person who feels proud experiences a boost to his self-esteem. He sees his position as in some respect comparatively better and so can take a more favourable view of himself. But he may think the respect in which his position is now better a quite unimportant one in his general scheme of values. He may, for instance, be proud of his precious snuff-box although being a snuff-box owner does not strike him as a matter of much moment. A person may be proud of something which he regards as relatively trivial and as having nothing to do with his commitments. What makes a person, if only temporarily, take a more favourable view of himself is wide-ranging and need not touch on his integrity. I said earlier that pride in all its forms concerns the status of the self. But what is included here under 'status' goes beyond his identity in terms of his commitments. 'Status' was explained in terms of a persons's norm of expectations, and these expectations cover areas of, to him, varying degrees of importance. In this respect pride and shame are not polar opposites: if 'status' includes but is not exhausted by expectations relating to the agent's commitments then the occasion for pride may be found anywhere in that area, whereas occasions for shame are restricted to what is seen at the time as centrally important.

It may seem that the contrast just drawn is not soundly based: it may be that as the emphasis in the discussion of shame has been on the moment of its occurrence while pride has been seen as primarily dispositional, the comparison is between features which are not analogous. It may be that on those occasions when pride wells up in a person, whatever he is proud of will at that moment also strike him as centrally important, and it is only later, when he thinks about the matter, that he recognizes its relative triviality. But whether or not this is the case, the difference between shame and pride in their respective relation to integrity rests ultimately not on this but on the difference in the way self-respect and self-esteem are related to integrity. Whether or not a person thinks favourably of himself has nothing to do with his integrity, whereas whether or not he can respect himself has. This is so because a person need not be conscious of his possessing or acting with integrity, he need pay no particular attention to himself and have no particular attitude towards himself.

Self-respect required both, that the person had certain commitments and that he was confident that by and large he had got his commitments right and was capable of living accordingly. It seemed possible that a person could have integrity and yet lack self-respect because he lacked the required self-confidence. It may be that he cannot have confidence in himself unless he can think well of himself. Self-esteem may be necessary for him to have self-respect. In that case, of course, self-esteem and self-respect are interconnected. But the interconnection between them is in an area which does not touch that person's integrity. Self-esteem may be connected with self-respect in that it contributes to his having a sense of his own value. But this aspect of self-respect is itself independent of the agent's integrity, or is related to it only to the extent that a more secure sense of one's own value is a better protector of one's integrity.

Humiliation, like pride, is also not directly connected with integrity, and that for the same reason. When feeling humiliated a person realizes either that her good opinion of herself is unfounded, or that her belief that she commands the good opinion of others is mistaken. Her belief that she is not, or is no longer, esteemed by others as she had supposed may affect her own self-esteem. But she may also retain her self-esteem if she believes these others to be mistaken. They do not give her what she deserves. Either experience may also affect her self-respect, whether it does or not will depend on what she needs to maintain her sense of her own value. Just as increased self-esteem may have a favourable effect on a person's self-respect, so a blow to her self-esteem may undermine her self-respect. But the fact that it is here a matter of loss and not, as in pride, a matter of gain in self-esteem will make the impact on the person's integrity a more serious one. If the occasion of her humiliation is the shattering of the favourable view she had been taking of herself as having certain commitments and acting in certain ways, then confidence in her values may be shaken to such a degree that it may well constitute a threat to her integrity.

It is after all not surprising that it should be the 'negative' emotions like shame and guilt and possibly humiliation which are more importantly connected with a person's integrity than is a 'positive' emotion like pride. The self in terms of a web of commitments, though not static, may still be thought of as being in a state of equilibrium, if all is well with these commitments. Such an equilibrium can be affected only by something going wrong; it can be upset, but it cannot be improved. So pride has here no role to play. Guilt and shame, however, have: the beliefs which identify these emotions are concerned with a disturbance in the equilibrium. But this does not mean that in experiencing them the agent just takes a certain view of herself. The experience is not wholly cognitive. She is not related to her integrity as a detached observer is to some independent state of affairs. The occurrence of the thoughts and the feeling-reactions which constitute guilt or shame itself has an effect on the self.

The experiencing of these emotions affects the self in that it operates as a pressure to maintain or return to the equilibrium. In feeling guilt or shame the agent sees the equilibrium being disturbed or threatened in different ways, and the painfulness of the emotions is occasioned by the perceived contrast between what the agent has done and ought to have done, or by what she is and ought to be. Within the person's scheme of evaluations the pressure exercised by them may or may not be properly channelled. False shame, for example, or irrational guilt, exert pressures to be a self which is not the agent's genuine self. A person experienced false shame on an occasion when she (perhaps only momentarily) accepted a standard that was alien to her. The pressure here is therefore destructive of the equilibrium which consists of her genuine commitments. Feelings of guilt may similarly be misdirected. Guilt is not false in the sense in which shame may be false, for what is thought to be forbidden will not be alien to the person concerned: it is part of a scheme of values which the agent accepted at any rate at some point, even if she now thinks differently. But guilt (like shame) may be irrational, i.e., it may be felt about something which the agent now judges not to be wrong at all, or which in the light of her general commitments she would so judge if she thought about the matter. The pressure of irrational guilt is as misplaced as is that of false shame: in implying an evaluation which is contrary to the agent's genuine commitments its pressure is a threat to the equilibrium rather than a push towards maintaining it.

From the agent's own point of view, then, genuine guilt and shame have a useful function to fulfil, whereas, as one might expect, these emotions are merely destructive if, given the person's evaluations, they are ill-founded. Although genuine shame or guilt are always constructive in the sense of being a pressure towards maintaining or returning to the equilibrium, they need not therefore be of equal value to the agent. Sometimes they may simply be frustrating, viz., if their occasion is a state of affairs the agent cannot do anything about, as when she feels shame at the circumstances of her birth. In such cases, perhaps, they may be taken as a reminder that evaluations are not data to be accepted as given but may themselves be in need of reassessment.

INDEX

Aquinas, Thomas, 51
arrogance, 47, 48, 50, 51, 101
Auden, W. H., 96-7
Austen, Jane, 36-7, 100n

Baier, Annette, 35n
belief, Ch. 1; explanatory, 2-4, 5, 6, 8, 9, 12-13, 20, 22-3, 24-5, 34, 35, 41, 64-5, 66-7, 69, 77; identificatory, 2-4, 5, 13, 20, 23, 24, 34, 35, 41, 64, 66, 68, 103, 104
Bettelheim, Bruno, 125-6
Bunyan, John, 82

Cavell, Stanley, 82-3
conceit, 48-50, 52, 101
corruption, 83, 125, 129, 133

Davidson, Donald, 3n, 5-6, 8, 11, 12, 13, 14, 35n., 42
desires, 112-14, 115, 116, 117, 118, 119, 120, 121, 124, 125, 126, 130, 132
Dickens, Charles, *Bleak House*, 74n.; *Hard Times*, 49-50; *Martin Chuzzlewit*, 95-6, 100

Eliot, George, 121-2
embarrassment, 69-76
emotion, Ch. 1; and reason, 2-4, 5-7, 8-10, 11, 14, 22; *see also* belief, explanatory; intelligibility of, 5-8, 11, 12-14; moral, 76, 77, 84, 86, 97, 100-1, 105, 107; *see also* guilt, remorse, shame; propositional, 5, 8; social, 74
Eschenbach, Wolfram von, 81n, 110n

fear, 2-3, 4, 6-7, 13, 135
forgiveness, 90, 105-6
Frankfurt, Harry, 111-12, 113, 118
Freud, Sigmund, 85n, 88, 96, 135n

Gaskell, Elizabeth, 133n
Goffman, E., 69n, 75n
guilt, Ch. 4; 1, 5, 16; and authority,

85-9; and integrity, 131, 134-5, 139-41; and pride, 135; and punishment, 89, 90, 92, 93, 107; and responsibility, 90-2, 93; and self, 95-6, 97, 98, 103-4, 134-5; and shame, 87, 89, 90, 91, 92, 94, 97, 107, 135-7; as moral emotion, 86, 97, 100-1, 107

honour, 54, 55, 56, 94-5, 109-11
honour-group, 55-6, 57, 58, 64, 81, 109-11
humble, 17-9, 36, 43, 51, 52
Hume, David, 1n, 5, 12, 53; *see also* pride
humiliation, 1, 8-12, 13, 14, 15, 18, 19, 26, 43, 49, 67-8, 78, 137, 139
hypocrite, 123-4, 129, 133

integrity, Ch. 5; and consistency, 114, 118; and control, 113, 116, 124, 125-6, 129-30; and honour, 109-11; and morality, 127-9; and practical reasoning, 113, 115-17, 118-21, 122, 124, 126, 128, 129, 130, 131, 134, 137; and responsibility, 119, 124, 126, 127; and sincerity, 114; and virtues, 109, 127; perverted, 95, 96; *see also* guilt, pride, shame

James, Henry, 42n, 45n
Joyce, James, 8-9

Kant I., 70n
Klein, Melanie, 102-3
Kolnai, Aurel, 105-6

O'Hear, Anthony, 58n

pride, Ch. 2; 1, 13, 16, 54, 63n, 67, 77, 78, 135-6; and achievement, 38-40, 41, 42, 46, 48; and beliefs, 20, 22-3, 24-5, 27, 32, 34-5; and comparison with others, 44, 45, 46-7, 48-9; and expectations, 37-40, 42, 43, 44-6, 138; and happiness, 42; and integrity, 50,